Separation of Church and State:
God's Churches: Spiritual or Legal Entities?

Jerald Finney

Copyright © 2009 by Jerald Finney

Separation of Church and State:
God's Churches: Spiritual or Legal Entities?
by Jerald Finney

Printed in the United States of America

ISBN 978-1-60791-341-2

All Scripture quotations are taken from the Holy Bible, *King James Version: The Holy Bible, 1917 Scofield Reference Edition,* Edited by Scofield, E.I. Stonehaven Press, public domain edition; *The Holy Bible, The Thompson Chain-reference Bible,* Compiled and edited by Thompson, Frank Charles. Indianapolis, Indiana: B. B. Kirkbride Bible Co., Inc. 1964.

www.xulonpress.com

Jerald Finney may be reached at 512-385-0761 (office) or 512-785-8445 (cell). E-mail address: jerald.finney@sbcglobal.net. Website: churchandstatelaw.com.

Contact Jerald Finney for information on speaking, seminars, consultation, and information on operating as a New Testament church.

Acknowledgements

First, all glory to the great God and our Savior, Jesus Christ. He saved me and started me on a new path. He, through the Holy Spirit, inspired me to write this book.

Many of God's people, too numerous to mention, have inspired me over the years since my salvation. However, as regards this book, especial thanks are due to Dr. Greg Dixon for placing his confidence in me, sharing his knowledge and expertise with me, and honoring me by asking me to be lead counsel for the Biblical Law Center. Had he not given me the opportunity to represent the Biblical Law Center, I would never have had reason to have written this and other books concerning the preeminent issue of separation of church and state.

Preface

Just as Christ "loved the church, and gave himself for it,"[1] a Christian should give priority to his relationship with Christ since God says that this relationship—not salvation of souls, good works, missions, or anything one does for his fellow man—is His top priority.[2] Jesus said, "If ye love me, keep my commandments."[3] The greatest commandment is to love the Lord with all one's heart, soul, mind, and strength.[4] If believers and churches do not love Christ with all their heart, soul, mind and strength, God contemns all else that they do.[5] Christ tells churches who have lost their first love, in spite of many good works, to "repent and do the first works; or else I will come unto thee quickly, and will remove thy candlestick, except thou repent."[6]

In order to apply biblical standards regarding the relationships between Christ and His children and churches, between Christ and civil governments, and between a church and the state[7], one must first study the Bible and then facts concerning civil law. A systematic study of God's Word and reality reveals that many churches have a relationship not only with our Lord, but also with the state. This grieves our Lord.

This book contains many facts from civil law as well as many statements and principles from the Word of God. The author cites all his sources so that the saved person who reads this book can check out the law, the facts, and the principles and make a decision as to how God feels about His churches incorporating, obtaining 26 United States Code (Internal Revenue Code) § 501(c)(3) status, or becoming a legal entity in any other way.

Studying this book will help Christians and churches in America understand how to apply the principles concerning the love between Christ and His churches to reality. Go to churchandstatelaw.com for more information of Jerald Finney and other books and resources.

---

[1] Ep. 5.25.
[2] See Jerald Finney, *The Most Important Thing: Loving God and/or Winning Souls?* (Austin, TX: Kerygma Publishing Co., 2008 (churchandstatelaw.com)).
[3] Jn. 14.15.
[4] Mt. 22.37; Mk. 12.30; Lu. 10.27.
[5] Song of Solomon 8.7; I Co. 13.
[6] Re. 2.2-5.
[7] See Jerald Finney, *God Betrayed, Separation of Church and State: The Biblical Principles and the American Application* (Xulon Press, 2008 (www.xulonpress.com) or Austin, TX: Kerygma Publishing Co. 2008 (churchandstatelaw.com)) for a thorough study God's Word, history, and law concerning the issue of separation of church and state. Readers unfamiliar with the concepts in *God Betrayed*, including the biblical doctrines, will find the book to be very challenging. It is not written for the casual reader, but studying the book is worth the effort.

Separation of Church and State:
God's Churches: Spiritual or Legal Entities?

CONTENTS

Chapter 1
Introduction

To understand the truth about "separation of church and state" one must first be saved; then, he must study and meditate upon the biblical doctrines of government, church, and separation of church and state. After mastering the biblical principles, the American believer is prepared to examine their applications in the United States. The author attempted to cover the entirety of the issues in a prior work.[1] A review of those principles will be presented in this introduction following a brief history of the issue of separation of church and state.

Two opposing doctrines regarding union of church and state operate within the "Christian" world. One teaches separation of church and state, and the other union of church and state. The false doctrine that combination of church and state will bring peace and unity on earth was advanced by the Catholic church in the fourth century, and was the basis for the horrible persecutions of tens of millions labeled as heretics for resisting the teachings of the church-state union. Protestant churches continued this doctrine. Puritans, Anglicans, and other Protestant denominations brought the doctrine to America where they continued to persecute dissenters, but a great theological warfare and debate within the colonies resulted in separation of church and state (not separation of God and state) as guaranteed by the First Amendment to the United States Constitution. America became the second civil government in history, after the colony of Rhode Island, to

---

[1] See Jerald Finney, *God Betrayed, Separation of Church and State: The Biblical Principles and the American Application* (Xulon Press, 2008 (www.xulonpress.com) or Austin, TX: Kerygma Publishing Co. 2008 (churchandstatelaw.com)) for a thorough study God's Word, history, and law concerning the issue of separation of church and state.

implement the true biblical doctrine of separation of church and state, thereby guaranteeing religious liberty. Nonetheless, the warfare continues, those who believe church and state working together will bring peace and unity are gaining momentum, and the end time harlot spoken of in the Word of God is within sight.

The false doctrine concerning union of church and state incorrectly spiritualizes the Old Testament. That view takes the position that Old Testament principles for the Jewish religion and the nation Israel, the only theocracy ordained by God, are to be applied to the church and the Gentile civil government within which that church operates.[2] Those rules which applied to the Jewish religion and Israel are applied to the church and the state.

True division of the "Word of Truth" teaches that God ordained both Gentile nations and the theocratic nation of Israel. The original plan for Gentile civil government was initiated by God at the time of the flood.[3] Man became responsible to govern the world for God. A civil government, as defined by God, is made up of men under God ruling over man in earthly matters. The primary God-ordained purpose of Gentile civil government is to control evil men thereby maintaining some degree of peace in this present world. Gentile civil government has authority to punish those who commit certain crimes against their fellow man and to reward those who do good.[4]

---

[2] See *God Betrayed* and Leonard Verduin, *The Anatomy of a Hybrid* (Grand Rapids, Michigan: William B. Derdmans Publishing Co., 1976) for a thorough study.

[3] Ge. 9.1-6. What God ordained at that time was not called civil government, but that is what it was. It was the first time God gave man authority over man. See MERRIAM WEBSTER'S COLLEGIATE DICTIONARY 504 (10th ed. 1995), and AMERICAN DICTIONARY OF THE ENGLISH LANGUAGE, NOAH WEBSTER (1828). The older definition recognized the biblical teaching that God did not intend civil government to be an all-seeing, all-defining, all-controlling, all-directing eye; and that God Himself, as the Supreme Authority, has given churches, individuals, parents, and authorities, in addition to civil government, rules and boundaries by which to govern themselves and others without the control of the civil government, except for violations of certain moral laws. See *God Betrayed*, Section I, Chapter I, especially pp. 6-7.

[4] See, e.g., Ro. 13.3-4; I Pe. 2.14; I Ti. 1.9-11.

God later called out a nation unto Himself—Israel, the only theocracy He ever ordained. Advocates of church-state union incorrectly apply Old Testament principles regarding the Jewish theocracy to the church-state or state-church in Gentile nations. They also apply the principles laid out for the Jewish religion in Israel to the New Testament church. Israel was indeed a true *"ecclesia"* or "church," but not in any sense the New Testament church—the only point of similarity being that both were "called out" by the same God. All else is contrast. When Jesus said to Peter, as recorded in Matthew 16.18, "That thou art Peter, and upon this rock I will build my church," He was speaking of something that had never before existed. The organization, doctrines, and purposes of this new and distinct type of *"ecclesia"* were all laid out by Paul in his epistles.[5]

The ultimate God-given purpose of both the New Testament church[6] and state or civil government is to glorify God, each acting under God and His principles, but neither acting with or under the other. However, the underlying purposes and jurisdictions of church and state are significantly different. The underlying purpose of the state is fleshly or earthly; and the underlying purpose of the church is heavenly or spiritual. God ordained churches to provide spiritual or eternal good. God gave nations earthly power to secure temporal benefits for mankind. The

---

[5] "This is he, that was in the church in the wilderness with the angel which spake to him in the mount Sinai, and *with* our fathers: who received the lively oracles to give unto us: (Acts 7.38)." "Israel *in the land* is never called a church. *In the wilderness* Israel was a true church (Gr. ecclesia = called-out assembly), but in striking contrast with the N.T. ecclesia." *Holy Bible, 1917 Scofield Reference Edition,* n. 2 to Ac. 7.38, p. 1249. A full refutation of the theology which advocates combination of church and state (Covenant Theology) is beyond the scope of this book. Covenant Theology spiritualizes or allegorizes Scripture. Thus, the Covenant Theologian incorrectly believes that The Jewish religion and the church are the same. *God Betrayed* addresses this in some depth.

[6] See *God Betrayed,* Part I, Section III, Chapter 4 for a discussion of some of the distinctions between church and state and church and Israel.

jurisdiction of a nation is earthly and that a church is spiritual.[7]

God gave neither the church nor the state authority to rule over or with the other. Christians are told to obey civil government as regards certain earthly matters, but Christians and churches are not to be under the civil government with regard to spiritual matters, which include many activities and actions as shown in the Bible.[8] God gave churches free will, and churches can choose, against His will, to disobey God and voluntarily work with, under, or over civil government when such an option is available.

Christ ordained the church: "And I [Jesus] say also unto thee, That thou art Peter, and upon this rock I will build my church; and the gates of hell shall not prevail against it."[9] God ordained a church under God, not a business under civil government or an entity that is to work with, over, or under the state. A church is a local autonomous body of believers; and, as such, it is a holy temple for the habitation of God through the Spirit;[10] is "one flesh" with Christ;[11] and espoused to Him as a chaste virgin to one Husband.[12] A church, under God, owes no allegiance to any tribunal in the universe, except to that of the Lord Jesus Christ unless she willingly and wrongly combines with civil government, and is the body of Christ of which He is the Head.[13]

Civil government does not meet the qualifications needed to rule over the church and those matters assigned the church by God. Civil government, as already mentioned, does not have the authority given it from God

---

[7] See *God Betrayed*, Part One.

[8] See Jerald Finney, *Render unto God the Things that Are His: A Systematic Study of Romans 13 and Related Verses* (Austin, TX: Kerygma Publishing Co., 2009)(go to churchandstatelaw.com for more information including ordering information).

[9] Mt. 16.15.

[10] Ep. 2.21, 22.

[11] Ep. 5.30, 31.

[12] II Co. 11.2-4.

[13] Ep. 1.22, 23; Col. 1.18, 24.

to oversee or rule the church. Since civil government is usually led by the unregenerate, it does not have the nature or wisdom to handle spiritual matters.

Christians do have such nature and wisdom, as proclaimed by Paul: "Having made known unto us the mystery of his will, according to his will, according to his good pleasure which he hath proposed in himself."[14] He made clear that only the born-again believer, led by the Spirit, was qualified to handle spiritual matters. Paul also asserted that rulers, "the princes of this world," do not possess spiritual wisdom, indicating that most leaders are not Christians (undoubtedly, almost all leaders, and almost all leaders of civil government when he wrote the above words, are not and were not Christians) and are blind to spiritual matters.[15]

Persecuted Christians down through the last two thousand years have understood this and therefore have refused, even under penalty of torture, imprisonment, and/or death to submit the church and spiritual matters to the ungodly—the state-church combination or the civil government.

The Holy Spirit did not come into every believer in the Old Testament as He does every born again person in a church:

"Summary of the O.T. doctrine of the Holy Spirit: ... (4) In the O.T. the Spirit acts in free sovereignty, coming upon men and even upon a dumb beast as He will, nor are the conditions set forth (as in the N.T.) by complying with which any one may receive the Spirit. The indwelling of every believer by the abiding Spirit is a N.T. blessing consequent upon the death and resurrection of Christ (John 7.39; 16.7; Acts 2.33; Gal. 3.1-6). (5) The O.T. contains prediction of a future pouring out of the Spirit upon Israel (Ezk. 37.14; 39.29) and upon 'all flesh' (Joel 2.28-29). The expectation of Israel, therefore, was twofold—of

---

[14] Ep. 1.9.
[15] I Co. 2.1-16.

the coming of Messiah-Immanuel, and of such an effusion of the Spirit as the prophets described. See Mt. 1.18, *refs*."[16]

A Christian can be godly, while a non-Christian can only have some degree of virtue. Once a person is born again, he becomes a new creature, a spiritual being who is instructed by God to walk in the Spirit. "Except a man be born again, he cannot see the kingdom of God."[17] "Except a man be born of water[18] and *of* the Spirit,[19] he cannot enter the kingdom of God."[20] "That which is born of the flesh is flesh; and that which is born of the Spirit is spirit."[21] "Therefore if any man *be* in Christ, *he is* a new creature: old things are passed away; behold, all things are become new."[22] After the Holy Spirit was first bestowed upon Gentiles in as recorded in Acts 10.44, "the normal order for this age was reached: [from that point] the Holy Spirit is given without delay, mediation, or other condition other than simple faith in Jesus Christ."[23] Prior to that, "the Gospels had been offered to Jews only, and the Holy Spirit bestowed upon believing Jews through apostolic

---

[16] *1917 Scofield Reference Edition*, n. 1 to Mal. 2.15, p. 981.

[17] Jn. 3.3.

[18] The water which is spoken of here is the Word of God. This is consistent with all of Scripture, and is specifically stated in the Bible. "Being born again, not of corruptible seed, but of incorruptible, by the Word of God which liveth and abideth for ever." 1 Pe. 1.23. Jesus, in talking to the Samaritan woman said, "If thou knewest the gift of God, and who it is that saith to thee, give me to drink; thou wouldest have asked of him and he would have given thee living water.... Whosoever drinketh of this water shall thirst again. But whosover drinketh of the water that I give him shall never thirst; but the water that I shall give him shall be in him a well of water springing up into everlasting life." Jn. 4.10, 13-14. "Husbands, love your wives, even as Christ also loved the church, and gave himself for it; That he might sanctify and cleanse it with the washing of water by the word." Ep. 5.26.

[19] John the Baptist said, "I indeed baptize you with water, but he shall baptize you with the Holy Ghost." Mk. 1.8. See also, Mt. 3.11 and Lu. 3.16.

[20] Jn. 3.5.

[21] Jn. 3.6.

[22] I Co. 5.17.

[23] *1917 Scofield Reference Edition*, n. 1 to Ac. 10.44, p. 1164.

mediation."[24] "While Peter yet spake these words, the Holy Ghost fell on all them which heard the word."[25]

The man who has not been born again, is a fleshly man, who walks in the flesh "according to the course of this world, according to the prince of the power of the air, that spirit that now worketh in the children of disobedience."[26] He is subject only to the law.

On the other hand one who is born again, a member of a church, a part of the body, is a heavenly man, and a stranger and pilgrim on the earth who is told to be led of the Spirit. The Word of God instructs the believer as to his walk. A Christian is told to walk in the spirit, not in the flesh.[27] He is told that if he is led of the Spirit, he is not subject to the law.[28] God quickens those whom He saves in Christ, loves them, raises them up to sit in "heavenly places in Christ Jesus,"[29] and blesses them "with all spiritual blessings in heavenly places."[30]

The word "heavenly" signifies that which is heavenly in contradistinction to that which is "earthly."

> "'The heavenlies' [or 'heavenly places'] may be defined as the sphere of the believer's spiritual experience as identified with Christ in nature (2 Pet. 1.4); life (Col. 3.4; 1 John 5.12); relationships (John 20.17; Heb. 2.11); service (John 17.18; Mt. 28.20); suffering (Phil. 1.29; 3.10; Col. 1.24); inheritance (Rom. 8.16, 17); (Rom. 8.18-21; 1 Pet. 2.9; Rev. 1.6; 5.10. The believer is a heavenly man, and a stranger and pilgrim on the earth (Heb. 3.1; 1 Pet. 2.11)." [31]

---

[24] *Ibid.*
[25] Ac. 10.44.
[26] Ep. 2.2.
[27] Ga. 5.16-25; see also, Ep. 5.1-17, Jn. 6.63, Ro. 8.1-13.
[28] This does not mean that he is not subject to the state in those areas where God has given the state jurisdiction. If he harms or kills another, for example, God gives the state jurisdiction to punish him. See, e.g. Ro. 13 and I Pe. 2. 13-14; I Ti. 2.8-11.
[29] Ep. 2.1-10.
[30] Ep. 1.3.
[31] *1917 Scofield Reference Edition*, n. 2 to Ep. 1.3, p. 1249.

The church is made up of believers. "And the Lord added to the church daily such as should be saved."[32] The church, made up of spiritual beings, is a spiritual or heavenly body whose ultimate purpose is to glorify God. A church, as the spiritual household of God, "is built upon the foundation of the apostles and prophets, Jesus Christ himself being the chief corner stone."[33] "The word 'spiritual,' found 23 times in the Bible, always means heavenly minded, godly, holy, never self-centered."[34] "Whether therefore ye eat, or drink, or whatsoever ye do, do all to the glory of God."[35] A church, as the spiritual body of Christ, is to be subject to Christ, the Head of the body, in all things.[36]

Spiritual matters include all things involving a church, such as sending missionaries, preaching the Gospel, loving and helping others, and the use of property for the assembly of the saints. These matters are all related to the primary purpose of loving and glorifying God and the Lord Jesus Christ—the Head, the Husband, and the Bridegroom of the church—and loving our neighbor as well.[37]

A church is to sit together in heavenly places. God wants His churches to be run according to His spiritual principles. Sadly, as will be shown by facts in the following chapters, most churches are not run according to God's principles. A "church" run as a corporation, unincorporated association, corporate sole, or charitable trust with an Internal Revenue Code ("IRC") 501(c)(3) ("501(c)(3)") tax exemption is, to a greater or lesser degree, earthly. It is

---

[32] Ac. 2.47.
[33] Ep. 2.20; see also, I Co. 6.15-20, I Pe. 2.4-9, Ac. 4.11, He. 9.11, I Co. 3.9-17.
[34] Questions and Answers, *The Berean Call*, January 2007, Volume XXII, No. 1, p. 5, available at www.thebereancall.org.
[35] I Co. 10.31.
[36] Ep. 5.23-24, 30.
[37] See Jerald Finney, *The Most Important Thing: Loving God and/or Winning Souls* (Austin, TX: Kerygma Publishing Co., 2009)(go to churchandstatelaw.com for more information including ordering information)

designed and operated, at the very least partially, under the earthly rules of man which are contrary to the spiritual rules of God.

Combining the church with the state violates the biblical principle of separation that runs throughout the Bible.

> "Be ye not unequally yoked together with unbelievers: for what fellowship hath righteousness with unrighteousness? and what communion hath light with darkness? Wherefore come out from among them, and be ye separate, saith the Lord, and touch not the unclean thing; and I will receive you, And will be a Father unto you, and ye shall be my sons and daughters, saith the Lord Almighty."[38]

The following chapters give the reader many legal facts concerning incorporation and 501(c)(3) tax exemption. The author believes that the discerning believer will easily see—when he studies those facts and compares them to the biblical principles concerning church, state, and separation of church and state—that a church which incorporates, and secures 501(c)(3) status or becomes a legal entity in any other way, takes herself from God's perfect will, causes our Lord much grief, and contributes to the decline of true biblical Christianity. Ultimately, fewer and fewer souls are saved because of this compromise, because such churches lose the power of God. They have "a form of godliness but deny the power thereof."[39]

---

[38] II Co. 6.14, 17-18; see also, e.g., Ro. 6.16-22, 12.1-2; I Co. 6.9-20, 11.2-3; Ga. 1.4; Ep. 5.1-20; Co. 2.6-8, 3.1-25; Ph. 2.12-16; I Ti. 1.7-11; 1 Pe. 1.13-16, 2.11-12; I Jn. 2.15-17.
[39] II Ti. 3.5.

Chapter 2
Spiritual versus legal entities

A church can choose to be either a spiritual entity, an earthly entity, or a blend of those two entities. A New Testament church is a spiritual house only, not an earthly house or an earthly and spiritual house.[1] For a church to be a spiritual entity only and a New Testament church, the Lord Jesus Christ can be her only head.[2]

Doing one thing that combines church and state creates a legal entity. "Legal entity" means:

> "Legal existence. An entity, other than a natural person, who has sufficient existence in legal contemplation that it can function legally, be sued or sue and make decisions through agents as in the case of corporations."[3]

A legal entity is an earthly entity, designed and created by man and run according to man made rules and procedures. Incorporating makes a church a legal entity as does obtaining 26 United States Code (Internal Revenue Code ("IRC")) § 501(c)(3) ("501(c)(3)") status. A legal entity is an earthly, not a spiritual, entity.[4] A church which is a spiritual entity cannot sue or be sued because she is under the Lord Jesus Christ only and she has no legal existence and therefore no ties to the state. In modern day America, a church who becomes a legal entity is given absolutely no control over the state, but the state is given a good deal of control over that church.

---

[1] See, *e.g.*, I Co. 6.15-20; II Co. 6.16; Ep. 2.19-22; He. 3.6; 9.1-2, 11; I Pe. 2.4-6; *God Betrayed...*, Section II, Chapters 1-3, Section III, Chapter 4.
[2] *Ibid.*
[3] BLACK'S LAW DICTIONARY 893-894 (6th ed. 1990), definition of "legal entity."
[4] See *God Betrayed:* esp. Section II, Chapters 2 and 3, and Section III, Chapter 4 for a thorough discussion of spiritual entity and legal entity.

A church can become a legal entity in ways other than incorporation. For example, a church can become a legal entity by becoming a charitable trust or unincorporated association, applying for an Employee or Taxpayer Identification number, opening up a bank account, entering into a contract, etc.[5]

A church can also become a legal entity by holding property through incorporation or some other means. Although there is no precedent in Scripture for a New Testament church to own or hold property since such a church is a spiritual entity only, a New Testament church obviously must occupy real property to exist. "Real property" means: "Land, and generally whatever is erected or growing upon or affixed to land."[6] Hereinafter, the author, unless otherwise indicated, will use the term "property" in referring to "real property." By holding property in any manner, a church becomes a legal entity.

In America, a New Testament church may occupy property in a manner consistent with biblical principle in at least three ways. As will be shown in Chapter 7, a church may use both real and personal property held by a pastor/trustee, under a Declaration of Trust, for the benefit of the Lord Jesus Christ. Second, a church may use and occupy property if the owner gives the church permission to do so. Or third, a pastor/trustee, under a Declaration of Trust, may lease property to be used by a church for the benefit of the Lord Jesus Christ.

A pastor/trustee may hold legal title to real and/or corporal personal property[7]—which includes movable and

---

[5] See Chapter 6, *infra*.
[6] BLACK'S LAW DICTIONARY 1219, definition of "Real property."
[7] "Any kind of property, whether real or personal, freehold or leasehold, and any interest therein, whether legal or equitable, may be impressed with a trust. While the question of what property is made subject to a trust is determined by the terms of the trust, as a general proposition a property interest must be transferable to be the subject of an express trust." 76 AM. JUR. 2D *Trusts* § 247 (2007).

tangible things such as furniture, merchandise, etc.[8]—for the benefit of the Lord Jesus Christ through a Declaration of Trust without having created a legal entity. Such a trust relationship cannot sue or be sued. Although the pastor/trustee holds and distributes property for the benefit of the Lord Jesus Christ, the church holds or owns nothing and remains a spiritual entity.

This book will show that a church that holds real and/or personal property through a corporation has partially placed herself under the control of civil government, the sovereign of the corporate part of that church. Such a church operates with two heads. A church which obtains 501(c)(3) tax exemption has agreed to further limitations and controls by a secular head.

Civil government has no authority over New Testament churches, but it does have authority over incorporated 501(c)(3) religious organizations and other types of legal entities. Although the IRS recognizes that there is a distinction between churches and other types of religious organizations, a Moslem mosque, a Hindu temple, any type religious organization that meets the test laid down by the Internal Revenue Service ("IRS") is treated exactly as or better than an incorporated 501(c)(3) "church" is treated. The IRS and civil government by providing for incorporation, 501(c)(3) tax exemption and other types of devises have become involved with the exercise of religion; and, therefore, there is no "free exercise of religion" for churches which have been seduced by these government creations.

Through offering incorporation and later the 501(c)(3) tax exemption to churches, almost all of the states and the federal government opened the door; and most churches promptly entered and became incorporated 501(c)(3) religious organizations. Incorporation of churches was

---

[8] BLACK'S LAW DICTIONARY 1217, definition of "Property."

offered by states and did not violate the First Amendment because originally the First Amendment applied only to the federal government. However, the federal government was given some authority over the contracts created by incorporation because of the contract clause of Article I, Section 10 of the United States Constitution.[9] Churches sought incorporation partly to gain federal government protection of the contract with the state. The 501(c)(3) tax exemption ties churches to the federal government. State and federal governments have successfully tempted most churches to entangle themselves with civil government, thereby removing themselves partially or totally from under the Headship of Christ and placing themselves under the jurisdiction of the state of incorporation and the federal government.

Since the ratification of the First Amendment, the federal government has never forced a church to incorporate or get 501(c)(3) status. The Supreme Court still understands that the state cannot legally interfere with a church that does not willingly submit itself to the state.

In effect, as will be shown, the incorporation-501(c)(3) tax exemption is nothing more than a scheme designed to educate and control churches. The plan has worked. The state knows that it cannot control and educate a New Testament church. Civil government cannot tell a New Testament church what to believe, say, or do. The state has no control over such a church.

---

[9] See, e.g., Mark Douglas McGarvie *One Nation Under Law: America's Early National Struggles to Separate Church and State* "DeKalb, Illinois: Northern Illinois University Press, 2005).

Chapter 3
Incorporation of churches

A New Testament church cannot be organized according to the principles of both the Bible and civil law. Should a church organize, even partially, according to the principles of civil law, that church cannot also be in conformity to the principles of church organization laid down in the Word of God. For example, a church which incorporates is not a New Testament church. This is because a corporation is a legal entity created, designed, and organized by statute. A comparison of the laws governing incorporation with biblical principles makes this clear.

This chapter examines the civil law regarding incorporation of churches. American Jurisprudence Second (AM. JUR. 2D) is a highly regarded legal encyclopedia that summarizes law in America. AM. JUR. 2D looks at the Constitution, court cases, statutes, treatises, etc. in its analyses; and complete citations are included. The author will not give the citations in this book. The serious student may go directly to cited excerpts from AM. JUR. 2D to find and examine citations. American law says that:

"[a] corporation is an artificial being, invisible, intangible, and existing only in contemplation of law. As a mere creature of law, it possesses only those properties which the charter of its creation confers upon it, either expressly or as incidental to its very existence; these are such as are supposed best calculated to effect the object for which they were created. It is essentially the legal identity of a set of contractual obligations and entitlements.

"A corporation is not a natural person but rather an artificial person, that is, a legal fiction or a creature of statute.

"The attributes of a corporation may include the capacity of perpetual succession, the power to sue or be sued in the corporate name, the power to acquire or transfer property and do other acts in the corporate name, the power to purchase and hold real estate, the power to have a common seal, and the power to make bylaws for internal government. The incorporator's choice of a particular statutory framework for incorporation is not dispositive of the corporation's nature and status; the corporation's declared objects and purposes are determinative."[1]

The civil law makes clear that the sovereign of the corporation is the state:

"No corporation can exist without the consent or grant of the **sovereign**, since the corporation is a creature of the state and derives its powers by legislative grant. The power to create corporations is one of the attributes of **sovereignty**. There is no inherent right to conduct business as a corporation. The right to act as a corporation does not belong to citizens by common right, but is a special privilege conferred by the **sovereign** power of the state or nation. Until there is a grant of that right, whether by a special charter or under a general law, there can be no corporation. Any means of incorporation that a state sees fit to adopt are appropriate.

"The right to conduct business as a corporation, being a privilege, may be withheld by the state, or may be made subject to appropriate terms and restrictions. **Because the granting of the privilege to be a corporation and to do business in that form rests entirely in the state's discretion, a state is justified in imposing such conditions on that privilege as it deems necessary, so long as those conditions are not imposed in a discriminatory manner.**

"Reminder: The law of the jurisdiction in which a corporation is organized governs who may form a corporation, how it is formed, and the powers it will have after it is formed."[2] [Emphasis mine.]

"The right to act as a corporation is a special privilege conferred by the **sovereign** power, and until there is a grant of such right, whether by special charter or under general law,

---

[1] 18 AM. JUR. 2D *Corporations* § 1 (2007). AM. JUR. 2D is the abbreviation for American Jurisprudence 2d which is an authoritative legal encyclopedia used by lawyers and judges in researching the law and as authority in legal opinions.
[2] 18A AM. JUR. 2D *Corporations* § 156 (2007).

there can be no corporation. The existence and legal
characteristics of a corporation are matters governed by state
law. The commencement of corporate existence depends on
the terms of the statute under which the corporation is created.
As a general rule, the existence of corporations formed under
general laws commences when there has been a substantial
compliance with the conditions precedent prescribed by the
statutes. Frequently, the filing of the articles of incorporation
is specified as the act in the process of incorporation from and
after which the corporation exists as a separate legal entity."[3]
[Emphasis mine.]

"Sovereign" means: **"2 a** : possessed of supreme power
<[*sovereign*] ruler> **b** unlimited in extent : ABSOLUTE."[4]

Thus, according to civil law, by incorporating, a church
places herself under another head which is at odds with her
other Head, the Lord Jesus Christ. The sovereign state is at
least partially over an incorporated church which is an
invention of civil government. God is the only Head or
Sovereign over a New Testament church.

Since the 1819 *Dartmouth College* case,[5] which
solidified existing principles, the basic principles regarding
incorporation of churches have not changed. Black's Law
Dictionary comments on this are accurate:

A corporation is defined as "An artificial person or legal entity
created by or under the authority of the laws of the state. An
association of persons created by statute as a legal entity. The
law treats the corporation itself as a person which can sue and be
sued. The corporation is distinct from the individuals who
comprise it (shareholders). The corporation survives the death of
its investors, as the shares can be transferred. Such entity
subsists as a body politic under a special denomination, which is
regarded in law as having a personality and existence distinct
from that of its several members, and which is, by the same
authority, vested with the capacity of continuous succession,

---

[3] *Ibid.*, § 74.
[4] BLACK'S LAW DICTIONARY 1125 (6th ed. 1990), definition of "sovereign."
[5] *Trustees of Dartmouth College v. Woodward*, 17 U.S. (4 Wheat.) 518, 4 L.Ed. 629
(1819)(hereinafter *Dartmouth College*).

irrespective of changes in its membership, either in perpetuity or for a limited term of years, and of acting as a unit or single individual in matters relating to the common purpose of the association, within the scope of the powers and authorities conferred upon such bodies by law. Dartmouth College v. Woodward, 17 U.S. (4 Wheat.) 518, 536, 657, 4 L.Ed. 629; U.S. v. Trinidad Coal Co., 137 U.S. 160, 11 S.Ct. 57, 34 L.Ed. 640....

"[Corporations are classified as public and private.] A public corporation is one created by the state for political purposes and to act as an agency in the administration of civil government, generally within a particular territory or subdivision of the state, and usually invested, for that purpose, with subordinate and local powers of legislation; such as a county, city, town, or school district. These are also sometimes called 'political corporations.'
...

"Private corporations are those founded by and composed of private individuals, for private purposes, as distinguished from governmental purposes, and having no political or governmental franchises or duties.

"... [T]he fact that the business or operations of a corporation may directly and very extensively affect the general public (as in the case of a railroad company or a bank or an insurance company) is no reason for calling it a public corporation. If organized by private persons for their own advantage,—or even if organized for the benefit of the public generally, as in the case of a free public hospital or other charitable institution,—it is none the less a private corporation if it does not possess governmental powers or functions. The uses may be in a sense be called 'public,' but the corporation is 'private,' as much as if the franchises were vested in a single person. Dartmouth College v. Woodward, 17 U.S. (4 Wheat.) 518, 4 L.Ed. 629.... [Public corporations] are not voluntary associations [as private corporations are] and ... there is no contractual relation between government and the individuals who compose [the public corporation as there is with the private corporation and the individuals who compose it.]"[6]

The civil law of incorporation excludes God entirely as regards certain matters controlled by the contracts created by incorporation. God and His principles are not part of or

---

[6] BLACK'S LAW DICTIONARY 340 (6th ed. 1990), definition of "Corporation."

included in any of those contracts. A court will not consider biblical principles in a matter involving a contract dispute out of an incorporated "church." The court will only look to secular laws and cases. Instead of the agreements being between the covenanting entities and the covenanting entities and God, the agreements created are between the contracting entities (the members of the incorporated church), between each contracting entity and the state (each church member and the state), and between the entity thereby created and the state. Incorporation of a church creates a contract which places an incorporated "church" under the contract clause of Article I Section 10 of the United States Constitution: "The charter of a private corporation is a contract and entitled to protection under the provision of the Constitution of the United States prohibiting the several states from passing any law impairing the obligation of contract."[7] The contract clause reads in relevant part: "No State shall … pass any … Law impairing the Obligation of Contracts…."

"A corporate charter frequently is described as a contract of a threefold nature; that is, a contract between the state and the corporation, a contract between the corporation and its stockholders [or members if a private religious corporation], and a contract between the stockholders [or members] inter se. The charter also is spoken of as a contract between the state and the corporators."[8] The result of this contract is "an artificial person or legal entity created by or under the authority of the laws of the state, an association of persons created by statute as a legal entity" which can sue and be sued. God is not included in the contracts created by incorporation, nor does God desire to be included. That contract is outside His

---

[7] 18 AM. JUR. 2D *Corporations* § 81 (2007).
[8] *Ibid.*

perfect will since He desires His churches to choose to remain under Him only.

Other contracts are created by the bylaws of the corporation: contracts between the members or stockholders of a corporation, and contracts between the corporation and its members or its stockholders.

The multiple contracts created by the articles of incorporation and the bylaws entangle the incorporated church with earthly concerns. Contract is a humanistic or enlightenment principle.

> "The idea of government remaining neutral over values coincided with the use of contract law as a means of restructuring society. Contract law accords the individuals to any bargain the right to assert their own goals, values, and priorities. The law enforces the bargain, not the values contained in it. Yet implicitly, contract law enforces individualism over communitarianism by its refusal to impose a communitarian ethic upon contracting parties."[9]

The contract clause has been used by civil government to control and attack the marriage of Christ and His church. The contract clause applies earthly principles to a spiritual entity. How? To answer succinctly, contract law leaves God and His principles out of the equation. Under contract law, two or more equal persons, alone and without God and His principles, form a contract as opposed to a biblical covenant in which God is an active party. A contract is an earthly agreement designed by man. Contract treats the parties as equal people with equal voices and God and His principles are excluded. Pursuant to laws devised by civil government, disputes between contracting parties are settled by the civil government.

---

[9] Mark Douglas McGarvie, *One Nation Under Law: America's Early National Struggles to Separate Church and State* (DeKalb, Illinois: Northern Illinois University Press, 2005), p. 86.

Many Christians, in seeking incorporation of a church, feel that by so doing a church and/or its members are gaining additional protection from lawsuits and from civil government. However, the corporate veil can be pierced, and individuals in a corporation can be sued. Furthermore, the contract of incorporation does not protect the church from all civil governmental interference with matters outside the contract:

> "Although a corporate charter is a contract that the Constitution of the United States protects against impairment by subsequent legislation, a legislature can neither bargain away the police power nor in any way withdraw from its successors the power to take appropriate measures to guard the safety, health, and morals of all who may be within their jurisdiction. Thus, the powers or privileges of a private corporation, although not subject to direct impairment, may nevertheless be affected by the operation of certain fundamental governmental powers, such as the police power and power of eminent domain. The legislature may, without impairing the obligations of a contract, by general laws impose new burdens on corporations in addition to those imposed by their charters when such burdens are conducive to the public interest and safety, notwithstanding the power to do so may not have been reserved in the charter. Moreover, the state and those acting under its authority have the right to require a corporation to incur expenses in order properly to exercise its rights and to use its property and franchises with due regard to the public needs. Corporations are subject to legislative control equally with natural persons -- that is, they may be controlled in all matters coming within the general range of legislative authority, subject to the limitation of not impairing the obligation of contracts and provided the essential franchise is not taken without compensation."[10]

The corporation is established under a charter from the civil government and conclusively established by filing articles of incorporation:

---

[10] 18 AM. JUR. 2D *Corporations* § 83 (2007).

"A charter is an instrument or authority from the **sovereign** power bestowing rights or privileges; therefore, with regard to corporations, the term is correctly used in its limited sense only with reference to special incorporation by act of the legislature. The creation of a corporate entity is conclusively established by filing of articles of incorporation. Legislation confers corporate power through general or special statutes.

"Observation: The laws, whether constitutional or statutory, of the state where a corporation is organized, enter into, and become part of, its articles of incorporation or charter so that the charter of a corporation organized under a general law consists of its articles of incorporation and the laws applicable thereto. Only those statutes that in some way are intended to grant or restrict the powers of a corporation, however, become a part of the corporate charter."[11]

"Those who seek and obtain the benefit of a charter of incorporation must take the benefit under the conditions and with the burdens prescribed by the laws, whether in the Constitution, in general laws, or in the charter itself. A corporation accepting a charter consents to be bound by all of its provisions and conditions and cannot complain of the enforcement of any of such provisions and conditions, if, by a fair reading of the language, the enforcement in the particular manner is authorized. A state granting a charter of incorporation may define strictly and limit the uses of the corporate property necessary to the exercise of the powers granted. The state, however, may not enforce any part of a charter that is repugnant to the Federal Constitution."[12]

"Where there is a conflict between a corporate charter and the constitution and statutes under which it is issued, the charter must yield to the constitution and statutes. With respect to matters to which statutes do not apply, the articles of incorporation of a corporation are its fundamental and organic law."[13]

"The articles of incorporation establish a corporation's purposes and manner of governance."[14] "The contents of articles or certificates of incorporation are commonly

---

[11] *Ibid.*, § 78.
[12] *Ibid.*, § 79.
[13] *Ibid.*, § 80.
[14] 18A AM. JUR. 2D *Corporations* § 171 (2007).

specified by a state's corporation statutes. Statutory requirements as to the form and content of the articles or certificate must be substantially followed, and the courts have not hesitated to declare an attempted incorporation invalid for failure to do so."[15]

As **sovereign**, the state has ultimate authority in interpreting the articles of incorporation.

> "Because a corporation's charter embodies a contract between the state and the corporation, the corporation and its shareholders or members, and a contract among the shareholders or members themselves, the courts employ general principles of contract interpretation when construing articles of incorporation or a certificate of incorporation This means that courts must give effect to the intent of the parties, as evidenced by the language of the certificate and the circumstances surrounding its adoption. The question whether a corporation's articles are ambiguous is one of law, and when determining the meaning of ambiguous provisions, a court will consider the history and surrounding circumstances to determine the parties' intent. The articles should be construed in their entirety. If there is a hopeless ambiguity that could mislead a reasonable investor, the language of articles of incorporation will be construed in favor of the reasonable expectations of the investors and against the drafter."[16]

The corporate church must also have bylaws. "The bylaws of a corporation are a contract between the members of a corporation, and between the corporation and its members, while the articles of incorporation constitute a contract between the corporation and the state, between the corporation and its owners or members, and between the owners or members themselves."[17]

> "A bylaw is a self-imposed rule, resulting from an agreement or contract between the corporation and its members to conduct the corporate business in a particular way. The bylaws

---

[15] *Ibid.*, § 173.
[16] *Ibid.*, § 171.
[17] *Ibid.*, § 261.

of a corporation are the private 'statutes' by which the corporation is regulated and functions. The charter and bylaws are the fundamental documents governing the conduct of corporate affairs; they establish norms of procedure for exercising rights, and they reflect the purposes and intentions of the incorporators.

"Until repealed, a bylaw is a continuing rule for the government of the corporation and its officers. Bylaws constitute a binding contract as between the corporation and its members and as between the members themselves...."[18]

The conflict of these rules regarding bylaws with biblical principles is obvious to the knowledgeable Christian.

A business or other organization is "incorporated either for the benefit of the public (a public corporation) or for private purposes (a private corporation)." An incorporated "church" is a private corporation.

"A corporation is to be deemed a private corporation, though it was created for the administration of a public charity, where the endowments of the corporation have been received from individuals. A nonprofit corporation organized pursuant to a nonprofit corporation statute is a private corporation, where it is neither controlled nor owned by the state nor supported by public funds. A corporation organized by permission of the legislature, supported largely by voluntary contributions, and managed by officers and directors who are not representatives of the state or any political subdivision, is a 'private corporation.' ... A corporation may have a double aspect according to the nature of the powers granted and exercised. If they were granted and exercised for public purposes exclusively, they belong to the corporate body in its public, political, or municipal character; however, if the grant was for purposes of private advantage and emolument, though the public may derive a common benefit therefrom, the corporation, quod hoc, is to be regarded as a private company.'"[19]

---

[18] *Ibid.*, § 258.
[19] 18 AM. JUR. 2D *Corporations* § 30.

As can be seen, according to civil law quoted below (and to God) an incorporated church is somewhat of a two headed monster.

> "In determining the threshold question of the applicability of religious corporations law, a court will look to the provisions of the corporation's certificate of incorporation as well as the actual practices of the organization as revealed in its papers.
>
> "A church society, by incorporating, does not lose its existence or become wholly merged in the corporation. The religious corporation and the church, although one may exist within the pale of the other, are in no respect correlative. The objects and interests of the one are moral and spiritual; the other deals with things temporal and material. Each as a body is entirely independent and free from any direct control or interference by the other.
>
> "**Thus, whenever there is an incorporated church, there are two entities—the one, the church as such, not owing its ecclesiastical or spiritual existence to the civil law, and the other, the legal corporation—each separate, although closely allied. The former is purely voluntary and is not a corporation or a quasi corporation.** On the other hand, a corporation which is formed for the acquisition and taking care of the property of the church, must be regarded as a legal personality, and is in no sense ecclesiastical in its functions."[20] [Emphasis mine.]

Of note in the above quote is the inference that a non-incorporated, non-501(c)(3) church which has not in any way submitted to civil government or made herself a legal entity does not subject herself or owe her existence to civil law and her objects and interests are only moral and spiritual. This is in line with biblical principle that a New Testament church is spiritual only and has no earthly legal attachments.

Thus, one can see that an incorporated 501(c)(3) church, since she is under two heads, gets part of her powers from God and part from the civil government. Part

---

[20] 66 AM. JUR. 2D *Religious Societies* § 5 (2007).

of the church, as a legal entity, can sue and be sued as to both earthly and some spiritual matters. For a church to put herself in such a position clearly violates biblical principles since a New Testament church herself is a spiritual entity only. Part of the church must have elected officers who conduct business meetings, meet statutory requirements, etc.

> "A church that sees fit to become incorporated under state law is obligated to conduct its business activities in compliance therewith, including governmental regulation of its employment relationships, so long as the employment does not depend on doctrinal matters. Religious corporations are governed by the same rules of law and equity as other corporations."[21] ...
>
> "Statutory provisions sometimes authorize the membership of a religious society to incorporate as an ecclesiastical body with the power to make bylaws governing the selection of church officials and prescribing their duties."[22] ...
>
> "A church incorporated for the promotion of a defined fundamental religious faith or doctrine cannot by amendment change its religious creed or faith except by the unanimous vote of its members."[23]

That an incorporated church is an artificial person and a separate legal entity has many ramifications.

> "The corporate personality is a fiction but is intended to be acted upon as though it were a fact. A corporation is a separate legal entity, distinct from its individual members or stockholders.
>
> "The basic purpose of incorporation is to create a distinct legal entity, with legal rights, obligations, powers, and privileges different from those of the natural individuals who created it, own it, or whom it employs....
>
> "A corporate owner/employee, who is a natural person, is distinct, therefore, from the corporation itself. An employee and the corporation for which the employee works are

---

[21] *Ibid.*, § 4.
[22] *Ibid.*, § 6.
[23] *Ibid.*, § 7.

different persons, even where the employee is the corporation's sole owner.... The corporation also remains unchanged and unaffected in its identity by changes in its individual membership.

"In no legal sense can the business of a corporation be said to be that of its individual stockholders or officers."[24]

"A corporation is a person within the meaning of the due process and equal protection clauses of the Fourteenth Amendment to the United States Constitution and similar provisions of state constitutions and within the meaning of state statutes."[25] "However, a corporation is not considered as a person under the First Amendment to the United States Constitution (religious liberty clause) or under the Fifth Amendment to the United States Constitution." [26] In other words, a corporate church has given up much of her First Amendment protections since she is now a legal, and not a spiritual, entity.

"[A corporation] has no right to refuse to submit its books and papers for an examination at the suit of the State....

"[T]he corporation is a creature of the State. It is presumed to be incorporated for the benefit of the public. It receives certain special privileges and franchises, and holds them subject to the laws of the State and the limitations of its charter. Its powers are limited by law. It can make no contract not authorized by its charter. Its rights to act as a corporation are only preserved to it so long as it obeys the laws of its creation. There is a reserved right in the legislature to investigate its contracts and find out whether it has exceeded its powers. It would be a strange anomaly to hold that a State, having chartered a corporation to make use of certain franchises, could not in the exercise of its sovereignty inquire how these franchises had been employed, and whether they

---

[24] 18 AM. JUR. 2D *Corporations* § 44 (2007).
[25] *Johnson v. Goodyear*, 127 Cal. 4 (1899), cited in Barbara Ketay, *Church in Chains*, p. 9. Barbara Ketay can be contacted at bketay@yahoo.com; website: www.libertyandyou.com.
[26] Ketay, p. 9.

had been abused, and demand the production of the corporate books and papers for that purpose."[27]

By contracting with the state through incorporation, she supposedly gains certain "protections" while giving up certain constitutional rights. While a corporate church must "obey the laws of its creation," it also has constitutionally protected rights[28] which are quite different and less effective than the rights she had while a spiritual entity protected by God and the First Amendment. A church which is not satisfied with God's liberty, provisions, and protections (which are implemented by the First Amendment) seeks incorporation. God is a far more strong and benevolent protector and provider than the state.

When a church is not a legal entity, that church cannot sue or be sued. One can sue a legal entity such as a corporation, but how does one sue a church which is "a spiritual house made up of spiritual beings offering up spiritual sacrifices, and not a physical house made by man?"[29] Individuals, including members of a New Testament church, can be sued for tortuous actions or tried for criminal acts, but a New Testament church as a whole cannot be sued or tried for criminal acts committed by a member or members of that church.

The purpose of the corporation is at odds with the God-given purpose of a church. Ultimately, the purpose of a church is to glorify God by submitting herself to her Husband in all things.[30] The basic purpose of incorporation allegedly is to increase the happiness of man by creating a "distinct legal entity, with legal rights, obligations, powers, and privileges different from those of the natural

---

[27] *Hale v. Hinkle*, 201 U.S. 43, 74-75; 26 S. Ct. 370; 50 L. Ed. 652; 1906 U.S. LEXIS 1815 (1906)(Although this case did not deal with an incorporated church, the opinion lays out general rules of incorporation which apply to an incorporated church).
[28] *See Ibid.*, pp. 74-75.
[29] *See* Sections II and III of *God Betrayed....*
[30] *See* Ep. 5.24.

individuals who created it, own it, or whom it employs...."[31]

A corporation and a church have different creators. Church members, under authority of and in conjunction with the sovereign state, create the corporation. The sovereign God supernaturally creates a church: Jesus said to Peter, "That thou art Peter, and upon this rock I will build my church; and the gates of hell shall not prevail against it."[32] "And the Lord added to the church daily such as should be saved."[33]

The organization of a church and a corporation are different. The incorporated "church" has "employees."[34] Even should the incorporated "church" call their "employees" ministers, the state looks at them as "employees," and the state is the sovereign of the corporation. A New Testament church cannot have employees and remain a New Testament church. Nowhere in the Bible can one conclude that a church is to pay anyone a salary. To do so makes that church a legal entity. Does the Word of God teach that God wants His churches to have "members," that He wants them to have "employees," or that He wants His churches to have both members and employees?

Whereas a church is to have pastors, teachers, and so forth, state laws which create corporations require the corporation to have officers such as president, treasurer, secretary, and so forth.

Ownership of a church and a corporation differs. "Members in a nonprofit corporation are the 'owners' of the corporation and generally play a role similar to

---

[31] 18 AM. JUR. 2D *Corporations* § 44 (2007).
[32] Mt. 16.18.
[33] Ac. 2.47b.
[34] By "employees, the author means those who "work" for the church and receive a set salary. Members of a New Testament church serve the Lord and live by faith. They cannot receive a salary from a purely spiritual entity.

shareholders in for-profit corporations."[35] As has been pointed out, Jesus Christ owns a New Testament church. Jesus stated that He would build His church. The incorporated "church" is partly owned, authorized, and built by God and partly owned, authorized, and built by Satan.

The corporation owns the property. "The members of the corporation are not owners of the corporate property; the corporation and its members are distinct parties. The corporation has an existence distinct, separate and apart from its members."[36]

An incorporated church must deal with all the government red tape that comes with incorporation. The incorporated church must now elect officers, hold business meetings, notify members of those meetings pursuant to statutory requirements, keep records, etc. All these secular activities take tremendous time, energy, and resources which could be used in pursuing the God-given purposes and activities of a church. The incorporated church which does not comply with statutory requirements is being dishonest and could face further problems from her sovereign state.

A corporation cannot be the bride of Christ, the wife of Christ. The incorporated part of an incorporated church is not the bride of Christ, the wife of Christ, but rather an extramarital illicit relationship existing alongside the marriage.

With the above information the author believes that any born again believer who loves the Lord and who has been saved any length of time at all should discern that Scripture contains no principle consistent with church incorporation or incorporation in general. In fact, everything about incorporation is anti-biblical.

---

[35] 18A AM. JUR. 2D *Corporations* § 609 (2007).
[36] Ketay.

The author has concluded—after a study of the Bible, history, and the law—that persecuted Christians in the early church and since until this day have understood that all they did in the spiritual realm was to be under the sole authority of the Lord Jesus Christ. They understood that they were married to Christ; and, because they have loved their spiritual husband and head, have honored that relationship at the cost of their earthly physical lives.[37]

---

[37] Persecuted Christians not only said, "I love you," to Christ. They showed their love by their actions. Saying I love you is easy and means nothing to Christ if not backed up by action. See, e.g., *The Most Important Thing*, Song of Solomon 8.7, and I Corinthians 13.

Chapter 4
Federal government control of churches through 501(c)(3) tax exemption

In the twentieth century, the federal government offered 501(c)(3) tax exemption to churches and religious organizations. 501(c)(3) status is unconstitutional in that it clearly violates the Religion Clause of the First Amendment to the United States Constitution, but churches have never challenged the constitutionality of the act as a whole.

The IRS exerts a certain amount of control over an incorporated 501(c)(3) "church." As has been pointed out, Scripture make clear that God wants no one else—especially the unregenerate—controlling, defining, and restricting his bride in any way. IRC terms set limits on and control the activities of the corporate 501(c)(3) religious organization.

501(c)(3) invites churches to seek a tax exemption from civil government, even though the First Amendment already has erected a "high and impregnable wall" of separation between church and state which forbids civil government from making any law, including any taxing law, respecting a New Testament church.[1] 501(a),(c)(3),(h) reads in relevant part:

"§ 501. Exemption from tax on corporations, certain trusts, etc.:

_____

[1] The history of the First Amendment makes clear that there is to be a wall of separation between church and state. See *God Betrayed...*, Sections IV and V. The United States Supreme Court has recognized this wall of separation and has stated that the Court will not allow the slightest breach. See, e.g., *Everson v. Board of Education*, 330 U.S. 1; 67 S. Ct. 504; 91 L. Ed. 711; 1947 U.S. LEXIS 2959; 168 A.L.R. 1392 (1947), reh'g denied 330 U.S. 855, 91 L. Ed. 1297, 67 S. Ct. 962 (while upholding the First Amendment wall of separation, the Court also added an additional meaning to the First Amendment which has been used to forbid recognition of God in practically all civil government affairs. See *God Betrayed*, Section V.)

"(a) Exemption from taxation. An organization described in subsection (c) ... shall be exempt from taxation under this subtitle [26 USCS §§ 1 et seq.] unless such exemption is denied under section 502 or 503 [26 USCS § 502 or 503]....
"(c)(3) Corporations, and any community chest, fund, or foundation, organized and operated exclusively for religious, charitable, scientific, testing for public safety, literary, or educational purposes, or to foster national or international amateur sports competition (but only if no part of its activities involve the provision of athletic facilities or equipment), or for the prevention of cruelty to children or animals, no part of the net earnings of which inures to the benefit of any private shareholder or individual, no substantial part of the activities of which is carrying on propaganda, or otherwise attempting, to influence legislation (except as otherwise provided in subsection (h)), and which does not participate in, or intervene in (including the publishing or distributing of statements), any political campaign on behalf of (or in opposition to) any candidate for public office....
"(h) Expenditures by public charities to influence legislation. (1) General rule. In the case of an organization to which this subsection applies, exemption from taxation under subsection (a) shall be denied because a substantial part of the activities of such organization consists of carrying on propaganda, or otherwise attempting, to influence legislation...."[2]

Notice that churches are not mentioned in 501(c)(3). It does mention, among other things, "[c]orporations ... organized and operated exclusively for religious ... purposes." Even the federal government thereby recognizes that the basic character of a church that seeks and obtains 501(c)(3) status has changed and that church has become a "religious organization." When a church incorporates, it becomes a corporation organized exclusively for religious purposes.

The state controls, defines, and instructs a corporate 501(c)(3) religious organization to a large degree. Control and definition go hand in hand. The federal government,

---

[2] 26 U.S.C. § 501(c)(3) (2007) in relevant part.

not God, defines "religious purposes" as to an incorporated church.

Under the IRS interpretation of 501(c)(3), to qualify for tax exempt status under 501(c)(3) religious organizations must meet the following requirements, i.e. abide by the following rules:

"1. must be organized and operated exclusively for religious, educational, scientific, or other charitable purposes,
"2. net earnings must not inure to the benefit of any private individual or shareholder,
"3. no substantial part of its activity may be attempting to influence legislation,
"4. the organization may not intervene in political activity,
"5. the organization's purposes and activities may not be illegal or violate fundamental public policy."[3]

Rules one through three above are stated in 501(c)(3). Rule four is also stated in 501(c)(3) and was added by legislation sponsored by Lyndon Johnson in 1954. The last requirement—"may not violate fundamental public policy"—is not from legislative law. This requirement was made law by federal court in the *Bob Jones University v. United States*, 461 U.S. 574 (1983). Thus, additional rules for 501(c)(3) churches are made by the legislative and executive branch as well as by the judicial branch. In *Bob Jones University*, the United States Supreme Court affirmed the IRS policy denying tax-exempt status to private schools with racially discriminatory admissions policies, because, according to the Court, those policies violated clearly declared federal policy. The Court concluded:

---

[3] IRS Publication 1828 (2007), pp. 3, 5. This and all IRS publications referred to may be accessed at irs.gov. IRS details on proscription #3 are on pp. 5-6 of IRS Pub. 1828. Just mentioning a candidate may violate proscription #4. Detailed guidelines with consequences of violation of proscription #4 are on pp. 7-11 of Pub. 1828. As to proscription #5, public policy is determined by the courts.

"Racially discriminatory educational institutions cannot be viewed as conferring a public benefit within the 'charitable' concept discussed earlier, or within the congressional intent underlying § 170 and § 501(c)(3)....

"This Court has long held the Free Exercise Clause of the First Amendment to be an absolute prohibition against governmental regulation of religious beliefs, *Wisconsin* v. *Yoder*, 406 U.S. 205, 219 (1972); *Sherbert* v. *Verner*, 374 U.S. 398, 402 (1963); *Cantwell* v. *Connecticut*, 310 U.S. 296, 303 (1940). As interpreted by this Court, moreover, the Free Exercise Clause provides substantial protection for lawful conduct grounded in religious belief, see *Wisconsin* v. *Yoder, supra*, at 220; *Thomas* v. *Review Board of Indiana Employment Security Div.*, 450 U.S. 707 (1981); *Sherbert* v. *Verner, supra*, at 402-403. However, '[not] all burdens on religion are unconstitutional.... The state may justify a limitation on religious liberty by showing that it is essential to accomplish an overriding governmental interest.'

"On occasion this Court has found certain governmental interests so compelling as to allow even regulations prohibiting religiously based conduct. The governmental interest at stake here is compelling.

"[The Court noted:] We deal here only with religious *schools* -- not with churches or other purely religious institutions; here, the governmental interest is in denying public support to racial discrimination in education.
[The Court also stated:] "The IRS policy at issue here is founded on a 'neutral, secular basis,' *Gillette* v. *United States*, 401 U.S. 437, 452 (1971), and does not violate the Establishment Clause."[4]

Although *Bob Jones University* was limited to religious schools in that a church was not being attacked in that specific case, the same rationale that supported the Court's conclusions can also be applied to 501(c)(3) religious organizations, although more hurdles will have to be jumped especially as regards a corporate 501(c)(3)

---

[4] *Bob Jones University*, 461 U.S. 574, 598-599, 603-605, fn. 29 at 604; 103 S. Ct. 2017; 76 L. Ed. 2d 157; 1983 U.S. LEXIS 36; 51 U.S.L.W. 4593; 83-1 U.S. Tax Cas. (CCH) P9366; 52 A.F.T.R.2d (RIA) 5001 (1983).

"church." It is common knowledge that the IRS regularly attacks corporate 501(c)(3) "churches" for infractions of requirements of IRS regulation. On the other hand, the rationale of the court does not apply to the New Testament church which remains a spiritual entity protected by God and by the First Amendment.

God wants members of His body, the church, to decide what is spiritual and what is not. If His body messes up, He will take care of it. The IRS requirements require instruction, definition, and control. The IRS determines, subject to costly and time consuming court challenge, whether a restriction has been breached by a 501(c)(3) religious organization. These restrictions subject a religious organization to civil suit for violating a federal government law.

Fundamental public policy may be ruled by a secular court to be above biblical principle for the corporate 501(c)(3) church. Certain public policies can, do, and will conflict with biblical principles. It is the responsibility of the church, not the state, to determine biblical principle as to the doctrines of the church. A nineteenth century Supreme Court wisely observed:

> "The question, what is the public policy of a state, and what is contrary to it, if inquired into beyond these limits, will be found to be one of great vagueness and uncertainty, and to involve discussions which scarcely come within the range of judicial duty and functions, and upon which men may and will complexionally differ; above all, when that topic is connected with religious polity, in a country composed of such a variety of religious sects as our country, it is impossible not to feel that it would be attended with almost insuperable difficulties, and involve differences of opinion almost endless in their variety. We disclaim any right to enter upon such examinations, beyond what the state constitutions, and laws, and decisions necessarily bring before us."[5]

---

[5] *Vidal v. Gerard's Executors*, 43 U.S. 127, 198; 11 L. Ed. 205; 1844 U.S. LEXIS 323; 2 HOW 127 (1844).

New Testament churches under God—spiritual entities with no income and which hold no property—are non-taxable. 501(c)(3) religious organizations under civil government are tax exempt. New Testament churches are non-taxable, and the First Amendment which recognizes this biblical principle is codified in 26 United States Code (Internal Revenue Code) § 508 ("§ 508") (the codification of Public Law 91-172 ratified in 1969):

> "§ 508. Special rules with respect to section 501(c)(3) organizations.
> "(a) New organizations must notify secretary that they are applying for recognition of section 501(c)(3) status.
> "(c) **Exceptions.** [Emphasis mine.]
> "(1) **Mandatory exceptions.** Subsections (a) and (b) shall not apply to—
> "(A) **churches**, their integrated auxiliaries, and conventions or associations of churches."[6] [Emphasis mine.]

> Note. A church applies for 501(c)(3) recognition by filling out and filing IRS Form 1023.

§ 508(a),(c) says churches are excepted from obtaining § 501(c)(3) tax exempt status. In other words, churches are non-taxable; and, therefore, churches are an *exception* to the civil government requirement that certain organizations file for 501(c)(3) tax exempt status. Thus, even the federal government recognizes that a New Testament church is non-taxable.

If a church does not apply for exempt status, and if it is organized as a New Testament church, according to the First Amendment which agrees with the biblical principle of separation of church and state, the church is an *exception*, and the non-taxable status of that church must be honored.

If a church successfully applies for exempt status, the government is granted some jurisdiction over the church

---

[6] 26 U.S.C. § 508 (2007).

since the civil government now declares and grants an exemption.

> **"EXEMPT, *a.*** Free from any service, charge, burden, tax, duty, evil or requisition, to which others are subject; not subject; not liable to; as, to be *exempt* from military duty, or from a poll tax; to be *exempt* from pain or fear. Peers in G. Britain are *exempt* from serving on inquests.
> "2. Free by privilege; as *exempt* from the jurisdiction of a lord or of a court.
> "3. Free; clear; not included.
> "4. Cut off from. [*Not used.*]   *Shak.*"[7]

> **"exempt** ... **2:** free or released from some liability or requirement to which others are subject."[8]

> **"PRIV'ALEGE, *n.* ...**
> "1. A particular and peculiar benefit or advantage enjoyed by a person, company or society, beyond the common advantages of other citizens. A privilege may be a particular right granted by law or held by custom, or it may be an exemption from some burden to which others are subject.
> "2. Any peculiar benefit or advantage, right or immunity, not common to others of the human race. Thus we speak of national *privileges*, and civil and religious *privileges* secured to us by our constitutions of government....
> "3. Advantage, favor, benefit."[9]

In spite of the fact that biblically sound churches are non-taxable, many, if not most, churches line up to incorporate and to become 501(c)(3) religious organizations. Why do churches apply? People know the answer and so does the civil government. The IRS itself has published the answer:

> "IRS concurrence that a religious organization is indeed a church is the best protection for a donor that his or her contribution to the church is tax-deductible and will not be

---

[7] AMERICAN DICTIONARY OF THE ENGLISH LANGUAGE, NOAH WEBSTER (1828).
[8] WEBSTER'S COLLEGIATE DICTIONARY 406 (10th ed. 1995).
[9] *Ibid.*

challenged in an audit. This knowledge makes a church's fundraising efforts much easier."[10]

One reason God denies jurisdiction to the state over spiritual matters and restricts state authority to earthly matters has to do with qualification for determining the meanings of words. The interpretation of laws and regulations requires the defining of words. Employees of civil government are not qualified to determine the meanings of spiritual terms; but, by dealing with spiritual matters, such people are called upon to deal with spiritual matters and to determine the meanings of spiritual terms. They must determine the meaning of "religion," "religious," "church," and many other words. Since these employees are operating outside their realm of expertise, the outcome of their decisions on these matters will conflict with the biblical meanings of those words. In defining words, therefore, civil government officials intrude upon the jurisdiction of the church—the church is subjected to the state.

For example, what does the word "religion" mean? The word "religion" is used only five times in the Bible, and only once in a good sense:

> "Which knew me from the beginning, if they would testify, that after the most straitest sect of our **religion** I lived a Pharisee."[11] [Bold emphasis mine].
>
> "For ye have heard of my conversation in time past in the Jews' **religion**, how that beyond measure I persecuted the church of God, and wasted it: And profited in the Jews' **religion** above many my equals in mine own nation, being more exceedingly zealous of the traditions of my fathers."[12] [Bold emphasis mine].

---

[10] Peter Kershaw, *Hushmoney* (Branson, Missouri: Heal Our Land Ministries), p. 30, citing Michael Chitwood, *Protect Your Contributions* (referring to statement of IRS on p. 3 of IRS Publication 1828).

[11] Ac. 26.5.

[12] Ga. 1.13, 14.

> "If any man among you seem to be religious, and bridleth not his tongue, but deceiveth his own heart, this man's **religion** is vain. Pure **religion** and undefiled before God and the Father is this, To visit the fatherless and widows in their affliction, *and* to keep himself unspotted from the world."[13]   [Bold emphasis mine].

Thus, from a biblical perspective, religion in the good sense may be defined as:

> "2. Religion, as distinct from theology, is godliness or real piety in practice, consisting in the performance of all known duties to God and our fellow men, in obedience to divine command, or from love to God and his law. James i.
>
> "3. Religion, as distinct from virtue, or morality, consists in the performance of the duties we owe directly to God, from a principle of obedience to his will. Hence we often speak of religion and virtue, as different branches of one system, or the duties of the first and second tables of the law.
>
> "Let us with caution indulge the supposition, that morality can be maintained without religion. Washington."[14]

Since the Bible also teaches that there is only one true God, there can only be one religion in the good and true sense. This means that all other religions are bad and false. All other "gods" are actually no gods at all:

> "As concerning therefore the eating of those things that are offered in sacrifice unto idols, we know that an idol is nothing in the world, and that there is none other God but one. For though there be that are called gods, whether in heaven or in earth, (as there be gods many, and lords many,) But to us there is but one God, the Father, of whom are all things, and we in him; and one Lord Jesus Christ, by whom are all things, and we by him."[15]

> "What say I then? that the idol is any thing, or that which is offered in sacrifice to idols is any thing? But I say, that the

---

[13] Ja. 1.26-27.
[14] AMERICAN DICTIONARY OF THE ENGLISH LANGUAGE, NOAH WEBSTER (1828), definition of "RELIGION."
[15] I Co. 8.4-6.

things which the Gentiles sacrifice, they sacrifice to devils, and not to God: and I would not that ye should have fellowship with devils. Ye cannot drink the cup of the Lord, and the cup of devils: ye cannot be partakers of the Lord's table, and of the table of devils."[16]

Since there is only one true God, there is only one religion with power from God. Before one can know that one true God, one must know Jesus Christ, God the Son:

"Jesus saith unto him, I am the way, the truth, and the life: no man cometh unto the Father, but by me. If ye had known me, ye should have known my Father also: and from henceforth ye know him, and have seen him."[17]

The Bible, as pointed out above, recognized the Jewish religion. Members of the Jewish religion (and any other religion) who do not recognize the Lord Jesus Christ as sovereign God are false religions and have no piety or power from God. "And Jesus came and spake unto them, saying, All power is given unto me in heaven and in earth."[18] Judaism denies that Jesus Christ is God the Son. The Jewish religion, like all other religions except true biblical religion, is therefore a false religion. The IRS and the federal government have concluded that all religions are equal and have created a pluralistic code and nation.

Civil government officials are required by § 501(c)(3) to define "church." By providing that churches can become legal entities by incorporating and obtaining 501(c)(3) status, the civil government assured that the IRS and the courts would have to define "church" because first, a lot of true churches would seek to incorporate and get government declared tax exempt status; and second, many religious organizations would claim to be churches so as to

---

[16] I Co. 10.19-21.
[17] Jn. 14.6-7.
[18] Mt. 28.18.

obtain the benefits offered by civil government. As one court noted,

> "We hasten to emphasize that by its use of the term 'church,' Congress must have intended a more narrow classification than that embodied by a term such as 'religious organization.' Despite the lack of guidance from Congress, and in the absence of a more explicit regulatory definition of the term 'church,' we will continue our efforts to give a distinct meaning to this statutory classification."[19]

In attempting to define "church," the IRS has "given certain characteristics [14 criteria] which are generally attributed to churches."[20] The court has recognized that 14-part test in determining whether a religious organization was a church. The 14 criteria are:

"(1) a distinct legal existence;
"(2) a recognized creed and form of worship;
"(3) a definite and distinct ecclesiastical government;
"(4) a formal code of doctrine and discipline;
"(5) a distinct religious history;
"(6) a membership not associated with any other church or denomination;
"(7) an organization of ordained ministers;
"(8) ordained ministers selected after completing prescribed studies;
"(9) a literature of its own;
"(10) established places of worship;
"(11) regular congregations;
"(12) regular religious services;
"(13) Sunday schools for religious instruction of the young;
"(14) schools for the preparation of its ministers."[21]

---

[19] *Foundation of Human Understanding v. Commissioner of Internal Revenue*, 88 T.C. 1341, 1361; 1987 U.S. Tax Ct. LEXIS 75; 88 T.C. No. 75 (1987).
[20] IRS Publication 1828 (2007), p. 23.
[21] *American Guidance Foundation, Inc. v. United States*, 490 F. Supp. 304 (D.D.C. 1980).

"In addition to the 14 criteria enumerated above, the IRS will consider '[a]ny other facts and circumstances which may bear upon the organization's claim for **church** status.' Internal Revenue Manual 7(10)69, Exempt Organizations Examination Guidelines Handbook 321.3(3) (Apr. 5, 1982)."[22]

The most glaring inaccuracy in the IRS criteria used to decide whether something is a church is the omission of God's principles from the characteristics. Notice, for example, that one characteristic of the IRS church is "a distinct legal existence." As has been pointed out, a New Testament church cannot have a legal existence. When the natural man defines a church, he leaves God and His principles out; or, should he include God, he must have an incorrect conception and definition of God, since he does not know God. The natural man, as exemplified by the IRS characteristics of a church, overlooks the fact that Jesus is the one who builds and is the chief cornerstone of the church. If Jesus, and Jesus alone, is not the builder, there can be no church. Paul wrote, speaking to the church:

> "Now therefore ye are no more strangers and foreigners, but fellowcitizens with the saints, and of the household of God; And are built upon the foundation of the apostles and prophets, Jesus Christ himself being the chief corner *stone;* In whom all the building fitly framed together groweth unto an holy temple in the Lord: In whom ye also are builded together for an habitation of God through the Spirit."[23]

The results of the attempts of the courts and IRS to define "church" include: first, some of those "religious organizations" which are not "churches," but have sought to be recognized by the civil government as "churches," have been declared to be "churches" by the civil government; and second, New Testament churches which

---

[22] 88 T.C. at 1358.
[23] Ep. 2.19-22.

have sought and obtained incorporation and/or "tax exemption" have become legal entities and lost their status as New Testament churches solely under God.

The state provisions and actions derived and resulting from those provisions which allow incorporation and declaration of tax exempt status of churches and religious organizations demonstrate:

(1) the wisdom embodied in the First Amendment which recognized that the civil government is not qualified to "make [any] law regarding an establishment of religion, or [to prevent] the free exercise thereof."

(2) the undesirable consequences of deviation from the biblical principles that the church is a spiritual entity, the only spiritual institution ordained by God; the state is an earthly entity ordained by God to operate only within its God-given earthly jurisdiction;[24] and that neither the church nor state should be over the other, but God should be over both.

(3) that the federal government (and the states since the incorporation of the First Amendment by the Fourteenth Amendment) violates the First Amendment when civil government provides for incorporation and tax-exempt status for churches or any other religious organization.

Just one illustration of what can happen when IRS officials determine what constitutes a church within the meaning of IRC § 170(b)(1)(A)(i), follows. The threshold question in determining whether an organization is a church described in § 170(b)(1)(A)(i) is whether the organization qualifies as a religious organization described in § 501(c)(3). Using the 14-part IRS test to determine whether a religious organization was a church, IRS officials held that an organization with the following purpose as stated in its articles of incorporation and bylaws was a church: "[T]o establish an ecumenical church to help people learn to pay

---

[24] See *God Betrayed...*, Sections I-III, esp. Section III, Chapter 4.

attention, wake up, and discover what both Christ and Buddha referred to as one's true self."[25] The ruling stated:

> "The organization was established to develop an ecumenical form of religious practice, place greater significance on the modes of religious expression that would unify western and eastern modes of religious practice, place greater significance on the mystical or interior experience of religious truth than that of most western church denominations, and be more spiritually satisfying to members than other existing church organizations."[26]

In other words, the IRS determined that an organization whose purpose was directly contrary to the principles for a church laid down by the Lord in His Word was a church.

The civil governments in the United States, through offering incorporation and 501(c)(3) status to churches, have constructed a code that destroyed the New Testament standing of churches which choose to incorporate and get 501(c)(3) tax exempt status.

---

[25] Internal Revenue Service Private Letter Ruling 8833001, 1988 PRL LEXIS 1594.
[26] *Ibid.*

Chapter 5
The incorporation-501(c)(3) control scheme

Legal scholars who have studied the issue point out that the civil government knows what it is doing when encouraging churches to incorporate and seek 501(C)(3) status. Furthermore, civil government agencies are contemptuous of the ignorance of Christians. For example, the IRS flaunts the fact that the IRC provisions exempting churches from taxation and providing for certain controls over corporate 501(c)(3) "churches" are contrary to the First Amendment. The first words in the body of IRS Publication 1828 are:

> "**Congress has enacted special tax laws** applicable to churches, religious organizations, and ministers in recognition of their unique status in American society and of their rights guaranteed by the First Amendment of the Constitution of the United States." [Emphasis mine.]

The First Amendment religion clause says:

> "Congress shall make **no** law respecting an establishment of religion, or prohibiting the free exercise thereof...."[1] [Emphasis mine.]

Parts of the IRC violate the First Amendment Religion Clause because those parts constitute a law respecting an establishment of religion which invites churches to give up their protection from civil government control and their free exercise of religion. As pointed out by law and facts below, in this chapter, the relevant IRC sections constitute an unconstitutional exemption-control scheme that allows the federal government to not only control and define "church," but also to teach satanic principles to a church.

---

[1] U.S. CONST. amend. I.

Churches which are considering becoming or which have already become corporate 501(c)(3) religious organizations also rely upon secular and "Christian" lawyers for advice. Some examples of advice given by "Christian" lawyers and other Christians concerning church incorporation and 501(c)(3) tax exemption follow:

> "Incorporate and get 501(c)(3) status. As long as the preacher preaches 'the gospel,' the church can organize any way it wants to organize."[2]
> "Incorporate [and get 501(c)(3) status]. It is the 'path of least resistance.'"[3]
> "Incorporate [and get 501(c)(3) status]. Incorporation is not the same as accepting a license. 'License' means permission by competent authority to do an act which, without such permission, would be illegal. Incorporation is just a way to hold property."[4]

A few Christian lawyers give the following biblically sound advice to churches:

> "Do not incorporate and get 501(c)(3) status. There is no excuse for incorporating or operating as any other type of entity that violates biblical principles regarding separation of church and state. The Lord is grieved when His wife, the church, places herself, even partially, under another's jurisdiction."[5]

The authority of those attorneys who encourage churches to incorporate and get the 501(c)(3) exemption is either a false theology, human reasoning based upon a humanist philosophy contrary to principles in the Word of God, and/or a combination thereof. The outcome of their

---

[2] Untold numbers of preachers, deacons, "Christians" and the vast majority of "Christian" lawyers and law firms.
[3] *Clergy & Professional Tax Conference,* (1997) Michael Chitwood, p. 28, cited in Peter Kershaw, *In Caesar's Grip* (Branson, Missouri: Heal Our Land Ministries, 2000), p. 72.
[4] Christian Law Association and Attorney David Gibbs. Horrible logic and a lie about what a corporation really is. Both licensing and incorporating along with 501(c)(3) status violate biblical principle. Just because one is wrong doesn't make the other right.
[5] Biblical Law Center and Attorney Jerald C. Finney.

efforts has been not only one nation under man's law (not under God), but also one church under man's law (not totally under God). The author challenges anyone to back up their position with a correct interpretation of Scripture.

The ultimate results which have been visibly transpiring for many years are the gradual devastating erosion of the law, fewer people being saved due to the demise of New Testament churches and Christianity, moral awfulness, and political anarchy in America.

Corporate 501(c)(3) churches remain in, at best, a lukewarm state.

> "And unto the angel of the church of the Laodiceans write; These things saith the Amen, the faithful and true witness, the beginning of the creation of God; I know thy works, that thou art neither cold nor hot: I would thou wert cold or hot. So then because thou art lukewarm, and neither cold nor hot, I will spue thee out of my mouth. Because thou sayest, I am rich, and increased with goods, and have need of nothing; and knowest not that thou art wretched, and miserable, and poor, and blind, and naked: I counsel thee to buy of me gold tried in the fire, that thou mayest be rich; and white raiment, that thou mayest be clothed, and *that* the shame of thy nakedness do not appear; and anoint thine eyes with eyesalve, that thou mayest see. As many as I love, I rebuke and chasten: be zealous therefore, and repent."[6]

As a result of the adherence by Christians to false principles concerning the relationship between church and state, the church and God, and the state and God, America has seen a steady erosion in establishment clause jurisprudence. Another effect has been the demise of true biblical preaching and teaching in churches For example, biblical principles regarding many doctrines among which are the sovereignty of God, church, civil government, and separation of church and state is non-existent or in error.

---

[6] Re. 3.14-19.

Even though the state still recognizes that a church is different from other religious organizations, it does not know what a church is. For example, the Internal Revenue Service states:

> "*The term* church *is found, but not specifically defined, in the Internal Revenue Code (IRC). The term is not used by all faiths[.]*"[7]
>
> "*Churches and religious organizations may be legally organized in a variety of ways under state law....*"[8]
>
> "Unlike churches, religious organizations that wish to be tax exempt generally must apply to the IRS for tax-exempt status unless their gross receipts do not normally exceed $5,000 annually."[9]

Nonetheless, the state wants to control churches. Some legal scholars know what the civil government is up to with the incorporation-exemption-control scheme. For example, Richard Garnett, assistant professor at Notre Dame Law School, in a well-documented law review article wrote:

> "The imposition of a tax is, after all, an assertion of power and an 'application of force.'[10] The same is true of the decision not to tax, or to exempt from taxation.... The decision to exempt certain associations, persons, activities, or things from taxation presupposes and communicates the ability to do otherwise; definitional lines drawn to mark the boundaries of such exemptions implicitly assert the power to draw them differently.... My claim here is that the decision to exempt religious associations from federal taxation may reasonably be regarded as an assertion of power—the power, perhaps, to 'destroy'—over these communities, their activities, and their expression....

---

[7] IRS Publication 1828 (2007), p. 2.

[8] *Ibid.*

[9] *Ibid.*, p. 3; see also, IRC (26 U.S.C.) § 508, discussed *supra* at p. 389.

[10] Richard W. Garnett, *A Quiet Faith? Taxes, Politics, and the Privatization of Religion,* 42 B.C. L. Rev. 771, 772 (2001), citing Stephen L. Carter, *The Free Exercise Thereof,* 38 Wm. & Mary L. Rev. 1627, 1639 (1997)("It is the application of force, not the happenstance that one is able to apply it with legitimate authority, that generates the power that destroys the specialness of religion.").

"In other words, maybe the power to tax churches, to exempt them from taxation, and to attach conditions to such exemptions really does as Chief Justice Marshall quipped, 'involve the power to destroy' religion. Neither heavy-handed repression nor even overt hostility toward faith is required, but merely the subtly didactic power of the law. Government need only express and enforce its own view of the nature of religion—i.e., that it is a private matter—and of its proper place—i.e., in the private sphere, not in politics—and religious believers and associations may yield to the temptation to embrace, and to incorporate, this view themselves....

"It is an exemption-and-restriction scheme in which the government extends an invitation to 'religious organizations' to receive a tax exemption in return for allowing the government to interpret and categorize the expression and activities of the church.

"There is the danger that, having made their own the government's view of religion's place, now-humbled and no-longer-prophetic religious associations will retreat with their witness to the 'private' sphere where—they now agree—they belong, leaving persons to face the state alone in the hollowed-out remains of the public square....

"Still it strikes me that the Internal Revenue Code Section 501(c)(3)'s exemption-and-restriction scheme is noteworthy in the extent to which it invites government to label as 'propaganda' or 'campaign[ing]' what are, for religious believers and communities, expressions of their faith and responses to their calling. It is far from clear that this is an appropriate task for the liberal state....

"My concern ... is that the premises of the conditional exemption scheme, the labeling it invites, and the monitoring of distinctions it creates will tame religion by saying what it is and identifying what it is not, tempt religion to revise its conception of itself and of its mission, and convince religious consciousness to internalize the state's own judgment that faith simply does not belong in politics....

"[The tax exemption] is simply the government's way of paying churches not to talk about certain things, enforce certain beliefs, or engage in certain actions—in other words, it's the government's way of privatizing the church....

"By determining for its own purposes the meaning of religious communities' statements and activities, and by enforcing the distinctions it draws, government subtly reshapes religious consciousness itself. In other words, by telling religion what it may say, really is saying, or will be deemed to have said, and by telling faith where it belongs, government molds religion's own sense of what it is....

"[Certain pronouncements] led my colleague, Professor Bradley, to suggest in another context that '[t]he Court is now clearly committed to articulating and enforcing a normative scheme of 'private religion.' Indeed, he argues powerfully that the Court's post-*Everson v. Board of Education* cases 'are most profitably understood as judicial attempts to move religion into the realm of subjective preference by eliminating religious consciousness.' ... [T]he Court turned to privatization 'as the 'final solution' to the problem of religious faction.' Its ambition—not merely the unintended effect of its decisions—is not only to confine the potentially subversive messages of religion to a 'nonpublic ghetto,' but also to revise and privatize the messages themselves. Having acquiesced to judicial declarations that it is a private matter, and accepted that its authority is entirely subjective, religious consciousness is unable to resist the conclusion that its claims to public truth are 'implausible nonsense,' and therefore cannot help but concede the field of public life and morality to government....

"[T]his privatization of religion is not simply its institutional disestablishment or an entirely appropriate respect on government's part for individual freedom of conscience and autonomy of religion institutions. Nor is the claim only that the exemption privatizes religion by deterring political activism and silencing political advocacy by religious believers and communities. It is, instead, that the exemption scheme and its administration subtly re-form religion's conception of itself. Government evaluates and characterizes what churches say and do, and decides both what it will recognize as religious and what it will label as political....

"[P]rivatization of the church is its remaking by government and its transformation from a comprehensive and demanding account of the world to a therapeutic 'cacoon wrapped around the individual.' It is a state-sponsored change in religious believers' own notions of what their faith means and what it requires.... The government tells faith communities that religion is a private matter, and eventually, they come to believe it.

"And finally, the retreat of religious associations to the private sphere suggests an ill-founded confidence that government will not follow. But it will. The privatization of religion is a one-way 'ratchet that stems the flow of religious current into the public sphere, but does not slow the incursion of political norms into the private realm.'"[11]

How is the 501(c)(3) tax exemption-definition-control scheme implemented? Simply by invitation. The government extends an invitation to incorporated "religious organizations" to receive a tax exemption in return for allowing the government to interpret and categorize their expression and activities. In effect, this is, as to churches, an invitation which tests the biblical knowledge of churches and church members, especially pastors (as to God's biblical instructions in the area of church and state) and their love for the Lord.

The IRS does not hide the fact that the exemption-definition-control scheme is implemented by invitation. The IRS openly proclaims:

"Although there is no requirement to do so, many churches seek recognition of tax-exempt status from the IRS because such recognition assures church leaders, members, and contributors that the church is recognized as exempt and qualifies for related tax benefits.... Unlike churches, religious organizations that wish to be tax exempt generally must apply to the IRS for tax-exempt status unless their gross receipts do not normally exceed $5,000 annually."[12]

Most Christians do not know that churches are not required to obtain 501(c)(3) exemption, and that to do so violates biblical principles. Imagine how the Lord feels about those few churches who keep His Word and do not deny His name. To the church in Philadelphia, God wrote:

"I know thy works: behold, I have set before thee an open door, and no man can shut it: for thou hast a little strength, **and hast kept my word, and hast not denied my name**....

---

[11] *Ibid.*, pp. 772, 774-777, 779, 796-800 (citations omitted).
[12] IRS Publication 1828 (2007), p. 3.

Because thou hast kept the word of my patience, I also will keep thee from the hour of temptation, which shall come upon all the world, to try them that dwell upon the earth. Behold, I come quickly: hold that fast which thou hast, that no man take thy crown. Him that overcometh will I make a pillar in the temple of my God, and he shall go no more out: and I will write upon him the name of my God, and the name of the city of my God, *which is* new Jerusalem, which cometh down out of heaven from my God: and *I will write upon him* my new name."[13] [Bold emphasis mine.]

---

[13] Re. 3.8, 10-12.

Chapter 6
Spurious rational for incorporating: limited liability

Today, the most common reasons given by churches for incorporating and seeking 501(c)(3) status are (1) limited liability; (2) to allow a church to hold property; (3) civil government recognition of tax exempt status assures church leaders, members, and contributors that the church is recognized as exempt and qualifies for related tax benefits (For example, contributors to a church that has been recognized as tax exempt would know that their contributions generally are tax-deductible); and (4) convenience—it is easier to get a tax deduction for tithes and offerings given to an incorporated 501(c)(3) religious organization than for tithes and offerings given to a New Testament church.

This chapter will deal with the first reason, limited liability. Chapter 7 will cover the second reason, as well as methods for a church to hold property in a manner consistent with biblical principle; and Chapter 8 will cover the last two reasons.

Members of "churches" argue that incorporating protects their personal assets (1) from liability for the debts of the corporation, (2) from the torts and criminal acts of the corporation, and (3) from liability on contracts entered into by the corporation. Each of these arguments will be considered in light of biblical principle.

One may argue first that incorporating a church protects his personal assets from liability for the debts of the corporation.

> "One of the major attributes of the corporate form of organization is that it insulates shareholders from personal liability for the debts of the corporation.... As a general rule,

and in the absence of a charter, constitutional, or statutory provision to the contrary, stockholders are not liable as such for any of the obligations of a corporation. Because a corporation is an entity, separate and distinct from its officers and stockholders, its debts are not the individual indebtedness of its stockholders."[1]

Limited liability is not absolute.

"The general rule that shareholders are not liable for corporate obligations or conduct is subject to numerous exceptions. Shareholders may be held individually liable to prevent or redress fraud, to achieve equity, or to prevent the avoidance of a legal obligation or duty.

"If the corporation is a mere instrumentality or alter ego of the shareholder, the corporate entity will be disregarded, and the individuals owning the stock and the corporation treated as identical, with the result that such individuals will be personally liable for the acts and obligations of the purported corporation. The limitation of liability to the corporate assets must give way to imposition of personal liability if the actions of those in control of the corporation denigrate the purpose of limited liability, which is to encourage investment of risk capital. The fact that a corporation is undercapitalized is not sufficient in itself to establish personal liability of the shareholders.

"Corporate creditors may reach unpaid stock subscriptions, and if a corporation is liquidated, the shareholders are liable if, otherwise, they would be unjustly enriched by retaining assets of the corporation free from the debts of the corporation."[2]

What does the Bible say about debt and repayment of debts? First, neither a Christian nor a church should go into debt.

"Owe no man any thing, but to love one another: for he that loveth another hath fulfilled the law. For this, Thou shalt not commit adultery, Thou shalt not kill, Thou shalt not steal, Thou shalt not bear false witness, Thou shalt not covet; and if *there be* any other commandment, it is briefly comprehended

---

[1] 18A AM. JUR. 2D *Corporations* § 724.
[2] *Ibid.*, § 728.

in this saying, namely, Thou shalt love thy neighbour as thyself. Love worketh no ill to his neighbour: therefore love is the fulfilling of the law."[3]

The Bible does not say "owe no man any thing unless you have to borrow money to build bigger church buildings, gyms, bingo halls, sports fields and facilities, cafeterias, fellowship halls, and/or any other type structures for the church." Notice that the commandment not to covet is also included. Most importantly, notice the importance placed on love. Will a Christian who loves his neighbor seek to protect himself from debts he owes to others; debts which the Word of God instructed him not to enter into?

> "He that is faithful in that which is least is faithful also in much: and he that is unjust in the least is unjust also in much. If therefore ye have not been faithful in the unrighteous mammon, who will commit to your trust the true *riches*? And if ye have not been faithful in that which is another man's, who shall give you that which is your own? No servant can serve two masters: for either he will hate the one, and love the other; or else he will hold to the one, and despise the other. Ye cannot serve God and mammon."[4]
>   Mammon means: "Riches, wealth; or the god of riches. Ye cannot serve God and *mammon*. Matt. vi."[5]

Thus, churches which go into debt for buildings or anything else distort themselves and become servants of the lender and money, not servants of God. "The rich ruleth over the poor, and the borrower is servant to the lender."[6] Pastors of churches who are serving mammon will find that they fear to preach everything God has laid on their hearts because they might offend some, especially rich Pharisees, who might either leave the church and/or cause problems within

---

[3] Ro. 13.8-10.
[4] Lu. 16.10-13.
[5] AMERICAN DICTIONARY OF THE ENGLISH LANGUAGE, NOAH WEBSTER (1828), definition of "MAMMON."
[6] Pr. 22.7.

the church. Failure to preach the whole gospel is displeasing to the Lord.

Christians and churches are to seek godliness, not worldly riches.

> "Perverse disputings of men of corrupt minds, and destitute of the truth, supposing that gain is godliness: from such withdraw thyself. But godliness with contentment is great gain. For we brought nothing into *this* world, and *it is* certain we can carry nothing out. And having food and raiment let us be therewith content. But they that will be rich fall into temptation and a snare, and *into* many foolish and hurtful lusts, which drown men in destruction and perdition. For the love of money is the root of all evil: which while some coveted after, they have erred from the faith, and pierced themselves through with many sorrows. But thou, O man of God, flee these things; and follow after righteousness, godliness, faith, love, patience, meekness. Fight the good fight of faith, lay hold on eternal life, whereunto thou art also called, and hast professed a good profession before many witnesses. I give thee charge in the sight of God, who quickeneth all things, and *before* Christ Jesus, who before Pontius Pilate witnessed a good confession; That thou keep *this* commandment without spot, unrebukeable, until the appearing of our Lord Jesus Christ: Which in his times he shall shew, *who is* the blessed and only Potentate, the King of kings, and Lord of lords; Who only hath immortality, dwelling in the light which no man can approach unto; whom no man hath seen, nor can see: to whom be honour and power everlasting. Amen. Charge them that are rich in this world, that they be not highminded, nor trust in uncertain riches, but in the living God, who giveth us richly all things to enjoy; That they do good, that they be rich in good works, ready to distribute, willing to communicate; Laying up in store for themselves a good foundation against the time to come, that they may lay hold on eternal life."[7]

The above verses speak to the saved person who is the temple of God, and, along with other believers, constitute a church body. Nowhere in the New Testament can one find

---

[7] I Ti. 6.5-19

a single verse condoning a church seeking riches and real or personal property. Rather, Christians are to be content with what they have. They are not to go into debt. If they will do the jobs God has given them, lusting after real property and other worldly things will vanish from their hearts and minds.

> "*Let your* conversation be without covetousness; *and be* content with such things as ye have: for he hath said, I will never leave thee, nor forsake thee. So that we may boldly say, The Lord *is* my helper, and I will not fear what man shall do unto me."[8]

And as long as a church maintains her New Testament status and remains under Christ alone, she can own nothing since she is a spiritual entity. As will be shown, a church can utilize property in ways which conform to biblical principles.

The apostles, and true Christians in their church body down through the ages, have been careful not to seek worldly riches; and they preached the whole counsel of God no matter who was offended. Nothing was ever mentioned in the Word of God about the early church seeking real or personal property. Churches assembled on property, but churches did not own property. The goals of churches and individual Christians were spiritual, not earthly. Individual Christians, at times, even went further than required by biblical principles.

> "And all that believed were together, and had all things common; And sold their possessions and goods, and parted them to all men, as every man had need. And they, continuing daily with one accord in the temple, and breaking bread from house to house, did eat their meat with gladness and singleness of heart, Praising God, and having favour with all the people.

---

[8] He. 13.5-6.

And the Lord added to the church daily such as should be saved."[9]

Thus, a New Testament church should not go into debt and should occupy property in a manner consistent with biblical principles.

As to torts and criminal acts, the member of a New Testament church has the same status as the member of an incorporated church: should a member of either type church be directly connected to criminal or tortuous acts, that member is not insulated.

> "Stockholders are not ordinarily liable for the tortious acts of a corporation unless they participate in or aid the commission of such acts. An individual's liability for the tortious conduct of corporation depends upon that individual's acts, and not upon any theory of vicarious liability based upon the individual's status as an owner. For example, a stockholder is individually liable for constructive fraud committed by a corporation only if he or she had knowledge of and instigated the fraud.
> "Caution: The rule shielding shareholders from liability for a corporation's torts do not shield shareholders from personal liability in tort for their own misfeasance or nonfeasance, including liability for negligence; a shareholder may be liable if he or she is the central figure in a corporation's tortious conduct. For example, a shareholder may be held personally liable for negligent acts in managing and supervising the employees of corporation, if those acts are a contributing factor in causing an injury."[10]

A New Testament church cannot be and is not liable for the tort or crime of a member or members since she is not a legal entity. People in a New Testament church may commit and be held accountable for torts or crimes, but the church herself cannot commit a tort or crime. If only one or more in a New Testament church commit a crime or tort, the entire church cannot be charged or sued unless

---

[9] Ac. 2.44-47.
[10] 18A AM. JUR. 2D *Corporations* § 726 (2007).

everyone in the church was involved. A Christian is not exempt from being falsely accused of a tort and/or a crime; and a Christian can walk in the flesh and commit or participate in a tort and/or a crime if he so chooses.

A New Testament church will not be involved with all the worldly matters with which an incorporated "church" is involved and which give the incorporated church and its members and officers opportunities and temptations for wrongdoing. The member of a church who loves the Lord and has his eyes on spiritual, as opposed to material, matters will be more likely to love his neighbor and to behave in a pious manner. The member of a church should understand that not only the state, but also—and primarily—God, desires him to be liable for and make restitution for damages to another caused by his tort or crime or for any tort or crime with which he knowingly, intentionally, recklessly, or with negligence participates.

A person is not ordinarily liable on contracts entered into by a corporation in which he or she owns stock. However, if a stockholder makes a contract as an individual, he or she is liable.[11] "It has been held that shareholders [or members] are not liable for a corporation's violations of state or local statutes, ordinances, or regulations in the absence of proof of active participation in the management of the corporation or the wrongs. However, it has also been held that the purpose behind incorporating is not to protect those who control a corporation from answering for its criminal actions."[12]

"A shareholder may expressly guarantee a corporate obligation. A shareholder's contract unconditionally guaranteeing payment of the corporation's debts is not abrogated by negligence of the creditor that results in the debt not being discharged in bankruptcy. Whether a shareholder

---

[11] *Ibid.*, § 725.
[12] *Ibid.*, § 727.

has guaranteed the credit of the corporation so as to become personally liable on its obligations in a particular case is a question of fact for the jury."[13]

A New Testament church, being a spiritual entity, will not and cannot enter into any type of contract. Contract, as has been explained *supra,* is an enlightenment principle which is antithetical to biblical principle.

---

[13] *Ibid.,* § 730.

Chapter 7
Spurious rationale for incorporating:
to hold property

The Bible and reality reveal that a church, a spiritual entity, since the spiritual part of the Christian is still housed in an earthly body, must occupy an earthly space and, therefore, property when meeting. God has given no other alternative. "Not forsaking the assembling of ourselves together, as the manner of some is; but exhorting one another: and so much the more, as ye see the day approaching."[1]

Thus, a church has to make some type provision for property in order to be able to assemble together and exist. Originally churches many times met in a church member's house. Many churches in America today have jumped to unbiblical conclusions as to how to possess property upon which to meet. Nowhere in the Bible can one infer that a building or property is a church.[2] Nowhere in the New Testament is there any indication that a church owned property. Nowhere does the Bible mention that the first churches owned property or that the Lord told churches to own property. This is because a New Testament church, under God only, is a spiritual body which cannot own property. By owning property, a church violates biblical principle, becomes a legal entity, entangles herself with earthly matters, and ceases to be a New Testament church.

Property in general includes money. New Testament churches did not hold money. Individuals in New Testament churches gave money to support pastors and for other purposes. But nowhere was there any indication that churches themselves held property of any kind.

---

[1] He. 10.25.
[2] See *God Betrayed...*, Section II.

The Great Commission says, "Go ye therefore, and teach all nations, baptizing them in the name of the Father, and of the Son, and of the Holy Ghost[.]"[3] Christ did not bring people into the temple or synagogue. Evangelism occurs outside the meeting place. Christians meet together for the preaching of the Word of God, for worshipping the Lord, for baptisms and for the Lord's Supper. There they are uplifted and prepared to go into the World to evangelize. The church which is doing what God desires is in the world where she is a light to those who are lost, not under a bushel where her light is hidden. New churches must go out into the world where they can be a light, so they meet in storefronts or other rented spaces. Maybe new churches grow because they have to go into the world.

Jesus told church members that they would "be witnesses unto [Him] both in Jerusalem, and in all Judaea, and in Samaria, and unto the uttermost part of the earth."[4] He said nothing about them getting big buildings or property. None of the conversions in the New Testament occurred in a church building, nor were the lost or new converts ever invited to a church building. Rather, "the Lord added to the church daily such as should be saved."[5] "[T]here was a great persecution of the church which was at Jerusalem; and they were all scattered abroad throughout the regions of Judaea, and Samaria, except the apostles.... Therefore they that were scattered abroad went every where preaching the word."[6] Everywhere Christians went, they preached the Word publicly. Never was any concern for property, real or personal, expressed. Again, this is because churches are spiritual, not earthly.

All property is connected with civil government through a title. Someone must hold legal title to the

---

[3] Mt. 28.19.
[4] Ac. 1.8.
[5] Ac. 2.47.
[6] Ac. 8.1, 4.

property upon which a church meets. Since the church must possess property to exist, she should endeavor to possess property in a manner consistent with biblical principle.

The obsession with property, among other things, has caused churches to jump to unbiblical conclusions and join hands with the state. In the colonies and early republic many Baptist churches ignored Scripture and sought incorporation for several reasons. For a time, one reason for incorporating in Massachusetts was to be sure that religious taxes paid by Baptists would be returned to their ministers by parish or town treasurers. For some Baptists a more compelling reason was to enable a congregation (as opposed to a spiritual church body) to make binding contracts between its members and its pastor, thereby guaranteeing regular payment of a decent salary. Those Baptists obviously cared little for the teaching of Scripture concerning contract and the manner in which a church was to provide for her pastor. In addition, incorporation gave all persons in the congregation the right to vote on building or repairing a meetinghouse. Some Baptists argued that incorporation was necessary to hold property or endowment funds in the name of the church.[7]

Churches in America have options as to how they may utilize property without themselves holding property and violating biblical principles. Two biblically acceptable options for a church to occupy property are the leasing of property by the pastor/trustee under a Declaration of Trust, or, if possible, using someone's property at no cost.

Another means for a church to possess property is available in the United States. A pastor/trustee can hold property for the Lord Jesus Christ as beneficiary. A church can execute a Declaration of Trust which proclaims to the world that the church is placing property under the care of a

---

[7] See *God Betrayed...*, Section IV and Section VI, Chapter 3 for reasons some Baptists gave for incorporating in the colonies and in the early history of the nation.

pastor/trustee who will hold the legal, earthly title to the property for the benefit of the true and equitable owner of the property, the Lord Jesus Christ. The Declaration of Trust and necessary associated documents are in line with both secular law and biblical principle.

"Declaration" means: "Publication, manifestation; as the *declaration* of the greatness of Mordecai. Esth. X.; A public annunciation; proclamation; as the *Declaration* of Independence, July 4, 1776."[8] Declaration of Trust is defined as follows:

> "The act by which the person who holds the legal title to property or an estate acknowledges and declares that he holds the same in trust to the use of another person or for certain specified purposes. The name is also used to designate the deed or other writing embodying such a declaration."[9]

This type of Declaration of Trust does not create a charitable trust. This is important because the IRS recognizes that charitable trusts are creatures of the state, legally organized under state law, along with unincorporated associations, nonprofit corporations, and corporations sole.[10]

> "It has been said that trusts are generally divided into two main classes: private trusts and charitable trusts. A 'charitable trust' is one in which the beneficiary is a governmental entity or in which the purpose of the trust is to implement public welfare or convenience. The primary differences between a charitable trust and other private trusts are that a charitable trust may be perpetual, the denominated recipients of the trust income may be indefinite, and the intended beneficiary is the community itself. It has also been said that the fundamental distinction between private trusts and charitable trusts is that

---

[8] MERRIAM WEBSTER'S AMERICAN DICTIONARY OR THE ENGLISH LANGUAGE (1828) definition of "DECLARATION."
[9] BLACK'S LAW DICTIONARY 408 (6th ed. 1990) under definition of "Declaration." This definition is consistent with the definitions in more authoritative legal references such as AM. JUR. and C.J.S.
[10] IRS Publication 1828 (2007), p. 2.

> in a private trust, property is devoted to the use of specified persons who are designated as the beneficiaries of the trust, while a charitable trust has as a beneficiary a definite class and indefinite beneficiaries within a definite class, and has a purpose which is beneficial to the community. [11]

Holding property by a pastor/trustee, not by the church, for the benefit of the Lord Jesus Christ is according to biblical principle and is entirely distinct from the man invented anti-scriptural practice of holding property through incorporation. As shown below, this manner of holding property does not affect the organization of the church at all and does not place the church under the state in any way.

Incorporation can be distinguished from the holding of property by a pastor/trustee for the benefit of the Lord Jesus Christ in many ways which emphasize (1) that incorporation is unbiblical and (2) that the concept of holding property in trust for the benefit of the Lord is found throughout Scripture. *First*, unlike a corporation which is a creature of the state and which comes into existence with the consent or grant of the state, holding property in trust in this manner does not create a legal entity. The right to act as a corporation is a special privilege conferred by the sovereign power of the state or nation. On the other hand, God left property in trust to mankind to maintain it for His benefit. God Himself initiated the concept of holding property in trust. For a pastor/trustee to hold property in trust for the Lord Jesus Christ, the real and equitable owner of the property, is biblical.

The basic purpose of incorporation—to create a distinct legal entity, with legal rights, obligations, powers, and privileges different from those of the natural individuals who created it, own it, or whom it employs—is at odds with the purpose of a church which is to glorify God by

---

[11] 76 AM. JUR. 2D *Trusts* § 4 (2007).

remaining a spiritual entity and submitting herself to her Husband in all things. When a pastor/trustee holds property for the true beneficiary of all property, the Lord Jesus Christ ("For by him were all things created, that are in heaven, and that are in earth, visible and invisible, whether they be thrones, or dominions, or principalities, or powers: all things were created by him, and for him:"[12]) by executing a proper Declaration of Trust and other necessary documents, a church is not placed under the state because no legal entity is thereby created.

Secular law interprets "trust" in a manner consistent with biblical principle:

> "A trust is not a legal entity. A trust is not an entity distinct from its trustees and capable of legal action on its own behalf, but merely a fiduciary relationship with respect to property. A trust is not a legal 'person' which can own property or enter into contracts, rather, a trust is a relationship having certain characteristics."[13]

---

[12] Col. 1.16.

[13] 76 AM. JUR. 2D *Trusts* § 3 (2007). This concept of trust is not overruled by Black's Law Dictionary which defines "Entity" as follows: "A real being; existence. An organization or being that possesses separate existence for tax purposes. Examples would be corporations, partnerships, estates, and trusts.... 'Entity' includes corporation and foreign corporation, not-for-profit corporation, business trust, estate, partnership, trust...." BLACK'S LAW DICTIONARY 532 (6th ed. 1990). Black's Law Dictionary defines numerous kinds of trusts. For example, a business trust is organized for the business purpose of making money.

However, that definition definitely does not apply to the type trust relationship created by a Declaration of Trust by which a pastor/trustee holds property for the beneficiary, the Lord Jesus Christ. Black's Law Dictionary defines "Legal existence" as "An entity, other than a natural person, who has sufficient existence in legal contemplation that it can function legally, be sued or sue and make decisions through agents as in the case of corporations." BLACK'S LAW DICTIONARY 893-894 (6th ed. 1990). The trust contemplated by the author of this book, and as recognized by the law generally, only contemplates holding property by a pastor/trustee for the true beneficiary. No legal entity is thereby created.

Black's Law Dictionary is not the authoritative law. Sometimes it is wrong, or sometimes, as in regards to trust, it is partially wrong, or when taken in context of all it has to say on a subject, has combined some truth with error as to legal conclusions. Here, Black's is internally inconsistent and clearly overruled by more authoritative legal sources.

There is a caveat which, if biblical guidelines are followed, is inconsequential to a trust relationship in which a pastor/trustee holds property for the benefit of the Lord Jesus Christ. Modern civil law is beginning to treat a trust somewhat like a legal entity, but only so far as the relationship between the trustee(s) and the beneficiary or beneficiaries is concerned. An outside party still cannot sue a trust.

> "Observation: The Restatement states that increasingly modern common-law and statutory concepts and terminology tacitly recognize the trust as a legal 'entity,' consisting of the trust estate and the associated fiduciary relation between the trustee and the beneficiaries. This is increasingly and appropriately reflected both in language (referring, for example, to the duties or liability of a trustee to 'the trust') and in doctrine, especially in distinguishing between the trustee personally or as an individual and the trustee in a fiduciary or representative capacity."[14]

This caveat should be of little or no consequence unless members of a church violate mandate of Scripture and run to civil government to sue their pastor asserting that the pastor/trustee has violated his temporal fiduciary responsibilities. By suing their pastor, they violate biblical principle.

> "Dare any of you, having a matter against another, go to law before the unjust, and not before the saints? Do ye not know that the saints shall judge the world? and if the world shall be judged by you, are ye unworthy to judge the smallest matters? Know ye not that we shall judge angels? how much more things that pertain to this life? If then ye have judgments of things pertaining to this life, set them to judge who are least esteemed in the church. I speak to your shame. Is it so, that there is not a wise man among you? no, not one that shall be able to judge between his brethren? But brother goeth to law with brother, and that before the unbelievers. Now therefore

---

[14] *Ibid.*

> there is utterly a fault among you, because ye go to law one
> with another. Why do ye not rather take wrong? why do ye not
> rather *suffer yourselves to* be defrauded? Nay, ye do wrong,
> and defraud, and that *your* brethren."[15]

Even should they violate biblical principles and sue their pastor, they still cannot sue a New Testament church, which is a spiritual entity only. Should members sue their pastor, they must do so as individuals. A New Testament church cannot bring suit, since it is not a legal or earthly entity.

Second, as has been shown, the state is sovereign over a corporation which is an invention of man and a legal entity. A trust relationship whereby a pastor/trustee holds property for the benefit of the Lord Jesus Christ under a Declaration of Trust, implements a principle God laid down in the Garden of Eden and which is seen throughout the Bible, and, as civil law agrees, does not create a legal entity over which the civil government has control. No principle in the Bible supports incorporation; rather, biblical principle is contrary to church incorporation and probably to any type incorporation.

Third, under a corporation, man does not hold property in trust for God. The corporation, a creature of the state, owns property. Under a properly drafted Declaration of Trust in conjunction with other properly worded documents, legal title to property is vested in a pastor/trustee for the benefit of the Lord Jesus.

The sovereign God owns everything—not only the land, but also everyone and everything. That ownership is implicit in the fact that He created it all.[16]

He clearly stated His ownership of all in His Word:

---

[15] I Co. 6.1-8.
[16] Ge. 1.

God said, "Now therefore, if ye will obey my voice indeed, and keep my covenant, then ye shall be a peculiar treasure unto me above all people: for all the earth is mine:"[17]

God said, "The land shall not be sold for ever: for the land is mine; for ye *are* strangers and sojourners with me."[18]

"But who *am* I, and what *is* my people, that we should be able to offer so willingly after this sort? for all things *come* of thee [God], and of thine own have we given thee."[19]

"The earth *is* the LORD'S, and the fulness thereof; the world, and they that dwell therein."[20]

God said, "For every beast of the forest is mine, and the cattle upon a thousand hills."[21]

"The heavens are thine [God's], the earth also is thine: as for the world and the fulness thereof, thou hast founded them."[22]

"The silver is mine, and the gold is mine, saith the LORD of hosts."[23]

Thus, when a church assembles together, God owns the land upon which they meet. The land is temporarily loaned to man for God's benefit, but God owns it. Although man has the temporal legal title to the land, God is the equitable owner. An equitable owner is "[o]ne who is recognized in equity as owner of the property, because real and beneficial use and title belong to him, even though bare legal title is invested in another."[24] "In a trust relationship, as distinguished from a 'contract,' there is always a divided ownership of property, to which the trustee usually has legal title and cestui [que trust] an equitable title."[25]

Mankind holds all property in trust for God. "Trust," as a noun, has been defined as follows:

---

[17] Ex. 19.5.
[18] Le. 25.23
[19] I Chr. 29.14.
[20] Ps. 24.1.
[21] Ps. 50.10.
[22] Ps. 89.11.
[23] Hag. 2.8.
[24] BLACK'S LAW DICTIONARY 539 (6th ed. 1990).
[25] 90 C.J.S. Trusts § 1, fn. 13 (2007). C.J.S., like AM. JUR 2D, is a highly respected, used, and cited legal encyclopedia.

"2. He or that which is the ground of confidence.

O Lord God, thou art my *trust* from my youth. Ps. lxxi.

"3. Charge received in confidence....

Reward them well, if they observe their *trust. Denham.*

"**8. Something committed to a person's care for use or management, and for which an account must be rendered. Every man's talents and advantages are a *trust* committed to him by his Maker, and for the use or employment of which he is accountable.** [Bold emphasis mine.]

"10. State of him to whom something is entrusted.

I serve him truly, that will put me in *trust. Shak.*

"11. Care; management. 1 Tim. vi.

"12. In *law*, an estate, devised or granted in confidence that the devisee or grantee shall convey it, or dispose of the profits, at the will of another; an estate held for the use of another. *Blackstone.*"[26]

"... 3. **a** : a property interest held by one person for the benefit of another. ... **5. a** (2) : something committed or entrusted to one to be used or cared for in the interest of another....—**in trust:** the care or possession of a trustee."[27]

American Jurisprudence 2d defines trust as follows:

"The fundamental nature of a trust is the division of title, with the trustee being the holder of legal title and the beneficiary that of equitable title. By definition, the creation of a trust must involve a conveyance of property.

"A 'trust' exists where the legal title to property is held by one or more persons, under an equitable obligation to convey, apply, or deal with such property for the benefit of other persons. A trust has been defined as a fiduciary relationship with respect to property, subjecting the person by whom the title to the property is held to equitable duties to deal with the property for the benefit of another person, which arises as a result of a manifestation of an intention to create it. The Restatement definition is similar, providing that a trust, when not qualified by the word 'resulting' or 'constructive,' is a

---

[26] MERRIAM WEBSTER'S AMERICAN DICTIONARY OR THE ENGLISH LANGUAGE (1828), definition of "TRUST."
[27] WEBSTER'S COLLEGIATE DICTIONARY, 1269 (10th ed. 1995).

fiduciary relationship with respect to property, arising from a manifestation of intention to create that relationship and subjecting the person who holds title to the property to duties to deal with it for the benefit of charity or for one or more persons, at least one of whom is not the sole trustee.

"Caution: A trust consists not only of property, but also of the trust instrument, the trust's beneficiaries and trustees, and the trust administrator [if any]."[28]

The principle of "trust" runs throughout the Bible. God owned all things—even the body, soul and spirit of man. God trusted man with all His earthly creation—including all property, real and personal—and left it to him in trust, as trustee or steward to be used for Him.

"Trustee" means, in relevant part:

"**1 a :** one to whom something is entrusted.... **2 a :** a natural or legal person to whom property is legally committed to be administered for the benefit of a beneficiary (as a person or a charitable organization)...."[29]

For example, Adam and Eve were trustees of the earth and all that was in it. In what some call the Edenic Covenant, God gave responsibilities to mankind.

"The man and woman in Eden were responsible: (1) To replenish the earth with a new order—man; (2) to subdue the earth to human uses; (3) to have dominion over the animal creation; (4) to eat herbs and fruits; (5) to till and keep the garden; (6) to abstain from eating of the tree of knowledge of good and evil; (7) the penalty—death."[30]

Although entrusted with all things, God gave mankind free will as to whether to carry out their responsibilities as trustees. The principle that nations—Gentile nations and Israel—and individuals were left in trust of land and all

---

[28] 76 AM. JUR. 2D *Trusts* § 1. (2007).
[29] WEBSTER'S COLLEGIATE DICTIONARY 1269 (10th ed. 1995), definition of "trustee."
[30] Ge. 1.28-31. This was pointed out on page 13 of this book.

things for the benefit of God runs throughout the Old Testament. This principle of trust continues to this day.

The Lord spoke of this concept of trust in at least two parables as recorded in the books of Matthew and Luke.[31] He spoke of an earthly master leaving certain amounts of his goods or money with his servants, according to their abilities. The more important parallel spiritual meaning was to the Lord and His servants. The master had an absolute right to his own goods, but he distributed to his servants to be used for the benefit of the master, the servants to be awarded according to their profitable use of the property entrusted to them. Some used the money productively and upon the master's return presented him with a profit. The property belonged to the master, and the servants were to use it for the master's benefit, not for their own benefit. Of course, they would be rewarded if they used the property wisely for the benefit of the master. One servant in each example returned only the original amount left in trust with them. The master instructed that the goods which he had left with the unprofitable servants be taken from them, and they were left with nothing. The profitable servants were rewarded by the master. In the story found in Matthew, the Master said, "[C]ast ye the unprofitable servant into outer darkness: there shall be weeping and gnashing of teeth."[32] Men, as servants of the Master are left in trust of all things for His benefit and will be rewarded or punished according to their use of His goods.

Timothy was a pastor, and a pastor has a special position of trust unlike other members of the body. Timothy was a trustee of a spiritual heritage: "O Timothy, keep that which is committed to thy trust, avoiding profane and vain babblings, and oppositions of science falsely so

---

[31] Mt. 25.14-30; Lu. 19.12-27.
[32] Mt. 25.30.

called:"[33] The Bible proclaims that pastors rule over the body. "Remember them which have the rule over you, who have spoken unto you the Word of God: whose faith follow, considering the end of their conversation."[34] "Obey them that have the rule over you, and submit yourselves: for they watch for your souls, as they that must give account, that they may do it with joy, and not with grief: for that is unprofitable for you."[35] "Salute all them that have the rule over you, and all the saints...."[36]

Biblically, a pastor must meet much more stringent God-given requirements than other members of the body:

> "This is a true saying, If a man desire the office of a bishop [pastor[37]], he desireth a good work. A bishop then must be blameless, the husband of one wife, vigilant, sober, of good behaviour, given to hospitality, apt to teach; Not given to wine, no striker, not greedy of filthy lucre; but patient, not a brawler, not covetous; One that ruleth well his own house, having his children in subjection with all gravity; (For if a man know not how to rule his own house, how shall he take care of the church of God?) Not a novice, lest being lifted up with pride he fall into the condemnation of the devil. Moreover he must have a good report of them which are without; lest he fall into reproach and the snare of the devil."[38]
>
> "For a bishop must be blameless, as the steward of God; not selfwilled, not soon angry, not given to wine, no striker, not given to filthy lucre;"[39]

---

[33] I Ti. 6.20.
[34] He. 13.7.
[35] He. 13.17.
[36] He. 13.24.
[37] "Having completed the treatise of doctrine and of the manner of handling of it, as well also of public prayer, he now in the third place comes to the persons themselves, speaking first of pastors...." *Geneva Bible Commentary* available on SWORDSEARCHER software. Go to www.swordsearcher.com for information on SWORDSEARCHER software.
"As [the term 'bishop'] is never used in the Scriptures with reference to *prelates*, it *should* be used with reference to the pastors, or other officers of the church; and to be a pastor or overseer of the flock of Christ, should be regarded as being a scriptural *bishop*." *Albert Barnes Notes on the Bible* available on SWORDSEARCHER software.
[38] I Ti. 3.1-7.
[39] Tit. 1.7.

These requirements are strict because the bishop is entrusted by God to "take care of the church of God."[40] He is a "steward of God."

> "The elders [pastors[41]] which are among you I exhort, who am also an elder, and a witness of the sufferings of Christ, and also a partaker of the glory that shall be revealed: Feed the flock of God which is among you, taking the oversight *thereof*, not by constraint, but willingly; not for filthy lucre, but of a ready mind; Neither as being lords over *God's* heritage, but being ensamples to the flock. And when the chief Shepherd shall appear, ye shall receive a crown of glory that fadeth not away."[42]

The pastor is an overseer of the church: "Take heed therefore unto yourselves, and to all the flock, over the which the Holy Ghost hath made you overseers, to feed the church of God, which he hath purchased with his own blood."[43] "Overseers" here refers to pastors.[44]

---

[40] I Ti. 3.5.

[41] "In this place the term πρεσβυτεροι, elders or presbyters is the name of an office. They were as pastors or shepherds of the flock of God, the Christian people among whom they lived." *Adam Clarke's Commentary* on the Bible available on SWORDSEARCHER software.

"That Peter means the officers, not the aged persons, is shown by I Peter 5.2." *The People's New Testament Commentary* available on SWORDSEARCHER software.

[42] I Pe. 5.1-5.

[43] Ac. 20.28.

[44] "*Overseers.* In **Acts** 20:17, they are called *elders;* here, *overseers,* which is, in the original, the same as the word rendered sometimes *bishops.*" *Abbott New Testament Commentary* available on SWORDSEARCHER software.

"Made you overseers – Εθετο επισκοπους , Appointed you bishops; for so we translate the original word in most places where it occurs: but overseers, or inspectors, is much more proper, from επι , over, and σκεπτομαι, I look. The persons who examine into the spiritual state of the flock of God, and take care to lead them in and out, and to find them pasture, are termed *episcopoi*, or superintendents. The office of a bishop is from God; a true pastor only can fulfill this office: it is an office of most awful responsibility; few there are who can fill it; and, of those who occupy this high and awful place, perhaps we may say there are fewer still who discharge the duties of it. There are, however, through the good providence of God, Christian bishops, who, while they are honored by the calling, do credit to the sacred function. And the annals of our Church can boast of at least as many of this class of men, who have served their God and their generation, as of any other order, in the proportion which this order bears to others in the Church of Christ. That bishop and presbyter, or elder, were at this time of the same order, and that the word was indifferently used of both, see Acts 20.17 (note)." *Adam Clarke's Commentary on the Bible* available on SWORDSEARCHER software.

The pastor then is obviously responsible to act as ruler, trustee, steward, overseer, and under shepherd of the church. Therefore, the Declaration of Trust should, to be biblical, name the pastor as trustee acting in trust for the beneficiary, the Lord Jesus Christ.

This does not mean that all men are not trustees. God has appointed every human being who has ever lived as trustee over himself, all that God has given him, his spiritual heritage, and his spiritual destiny. The earth was still God's, but man was told to care for and possess His earth. Mankind was "trustee" of the earth. The pastor is trustee of the church.

A declaration of the relationship between property held by a person for the benefit of Christ better serves its purpose if the terms "trust" and "trustee" as opposed to "stewardship" and "steward" be used. "Steward" means in relevant part:

> "1. A man employed in great families to manage the domestic concerns, superintend the other servants, collect the rents or income, keep the accounts, &c. See Gen. xv. 2—xliii.
> "5. In *Scripture* and *theology*, a minister of Christ, whose duty is to dispense the provisions of the gospel, to preach its doctrines and administer its ordinances. It is required in *stewards*, that a man be found faithful. 1 Cor. iv."[45]

The first meaning of "steward" is reflected in several passages of the Bible: Genesis 15.2, 43.19, 44.1, 44.4; I Kings 16.9; Matthew 20.8; Luke 8.3, 12.42, 16.1-8 (parable of the unjust steward). The last meaning is reflected in I Corinthians 4.1, 2 and Titus 1.7. "Stewardship" simply means "The office of a steward."[46] The terms "stewardship" and "trust," are distinct. The term "trust" better describes the desired relationship between the Lord

---

[45] MERRIAM WEBSTER'S AMERICAN DICTIONARY OR THE ENGLISH LANGUAGE (1828), definition of "STEWARD."
[46] *Ibid.*, definition of "STEWARDSHIP."

and the person who holds property for the benefit of the Lord Jesus Christ. Likewise, the meaning of the terms "steward" and "trustee," are distinct. "Trustee" better describes the position of a person who is to hold property or anything else for the benefit of the Lord. To understand this, carefully compare the definitions of "trust" and "stewardship" and "trustee" and "steward."

Luke 16.1-8 is the parable of the unjust steward. Following that parable, Jesus said,

> "He that is faithful in that which is least is faithful also in much: and he that is unjust in the least is unjust also in much. If therefore ye have not been faithful in the unrighteous mammon, who will commit to your **trust** the true *riches?* And if ye have not been faithful in that which is another man's, who shall give you that which is your own? No servant can serve two masters: for either he will hate the one, and love the other; or else he will hold to the one, and despise the other. Ye cannot serve God and mammon."[47] [Bold emphasis mine.]

Fourth, incorporation creates several contracts. The primary contract created by incorporation is a contract between church and state which places an incorporated "church" under the contract clause of Article I Section 10 of the United States Constitution. The articles of incorporation constitute a contract between the corporation and the state, between the corporation and its members (owners), and between the members (owners) themselves. Furthermore, the bylaws of the corporate church create contracts between the members of the corporation, and between the corporation and its members. All these contracts come under Article I, Section 10 of the United States Constitution, the "contract clause."

A Declaration of Trust creates no agreement or contract at all with or between anyone. Under such a Declaration, a trustee merely holds legal title to property for the benefit of

---

[47] Lu. 16.10-13.

the beneficiary, the Lord Jesus Christ. "Contract" is an agreement between two equal people which leaves God out of the equation. "Trust" is a biblical principle.

The members of the church, under the contracts of an incorporated "church," not only control the church property, they also control the spiritual direction of the church. Corporate trustees become the *de facto* rulers and overseers of the church. Members are beginning to realize and understand and exercise the power given them in the contracts entered into between themselves and the sovereign state, between themselves and the corporation, and between themselves. Dr. Greg Dixon explains:

"Fundamental Baptists have operated through a strong pastor/leader who has been able to control his board, but as David Gibbs, Jr. told me [Dr. Dixon] 20 years ago, 'We have a new breed of trustees now who are educated and understand their fiduciary responsibility.' Even after the Baptists gained liberty through the First Amendment, they held property by the Protestant method through lay trustees. In reality they had a church board contrary to biblical and Baptist polity which lasts till this day. These trustees are now firing preachers for cause. One old preacher in Ohio testified at a fellowship meeting and said that the trustees fired him on Saturday night and changed the locks, and he couldn't even get in on Sunday a.m. Another preacher in Colorado said that they fired him on Sunday p.m. and told him not to come back on Sunday night. They have power to call the police. They can violate the constitution and by laws, how can the preacher sue?

"Catholic clergy understand the effect of lay control of a 'church.' The Catholic laymen came to America without priests to begin with and started 'churches' including buying 'church' property and holding the property through the Protestant system with lay trustees. When the priests came they tried to take the property over through the corporation sole method as in Europe where the Bishop of the Diocese holds the property in his own name. The lay trustees didn't want to give up their power, but finally did; and the Catholic polity of corporation sole prevails to this day."[48]

Fifth, a corporation is established under a charter from the civil government and conclusively established by filing articles of incorporation with a state agency, the contents of which are commonly specified by a state's corporation statutes. Statutory requirements as to the form and content of the articles or certificate must be substantially followed. No such requirements exist for the drafting or filing of a Declaration or Trust. A Declaration of Trust can be drafted in any logical manner and need not be filed to establish the trust relationship. A Declaration of Trust in no way either subjugates a church to the state or creates any contract of any kind between anyone.

Sixth, whereas incorporation of a church creates a legal entity which subjects the church to the state, a pastor/trustee holding property for the benefit of the Lord Jesus Christ implements biblical principle in that the church remains a spiritual entity only. An incorporated church gets part of its powers from God and part from the civil government. It is under two heads: civil government and God. A church that sees fit to become incorporated under state law is obligated to conduct its business activities in compliance therewith, including governmental regulation of its employment relationships, so long as the employment does not depend on doctrinal matters.

A church which meets on property held by a pastor/trustee for the benefit of the Lord Jesus Christ and does not connect herself to the state in any other way is totally under God. No "business" practices or requirements in the operation of the church are initiated. By utilizing property held in trust by a pastor/trustee for the benefit of

---

[48] Dr. Greg Dixon is pastor emeritus of Indianapolis Baptist Temple. The information concerning the Catholic "church" is from John Cogley, *Catholic America* (Garden City, NY: Image Books, A Division of Doubleday & Co., Inc., 1960), pp. 200-203.

the Lord Jesus Christ, no entanglement of church and state results, no elections, board of directors, no officers, no employees, no business meetings, etc. are required since the civil government has absolutely no control over the affairs of that church.

Holding property in the recommended manner has additional benefits. Not only does holding property in this manner comport with biblical principles, it also lessens the chances that the property, and especially the buildings, will become idols. "Their idols *are* ... the work of men's hands. ... They that make them are like unto them; *so is* every one that trusteth in them."[49]   Finally, holding property in this way does not require that the church be structured as a business.

Thus, God instituted the concept of trust in the beginning, in the Garden of Eden. It is a biblical concept which is utilized in America today. Just because the law uses the concept and uses some of the same terms, does not mean that Christians can no longer use the concept and the term(s). For example, if adoption of biblical terms by the state means that thereafter use of those terms are prohibited by Christians, then Christians can no longer use the term "justification." A Christian who objects to the use of the terms "trust," "trustee," and "beneficiary" should never again use the term "justification" since that is a term utilized by the state.

Simply put, justification means "a reason to be found not guilty even though you are guilty." Biblically, all men are guilty before God. The only reason for a finding of "not guilty" before God will be salvation through the blood of Christ. Temporally, the criminal law provides justifications which allow guilty men to be found "not guilty." The Texas Penal Code provides: "It is a defense to the prosecution that

---

[49] Ps. 115.4-8.

the conduct in question is justified under this chapter."[50]
Self-defense is a justification for murder. Texas criminal
law further provides for self-defense: "… [A] person is
justified in using force against another when and to the
degree he reasonably believes the force is immediately
necessary to protect himself against the other's use or
attempted use of unlawful force."[51] "Justification" in
Texas law is a reason for your crime that provides a
defense. If the issue of a defense is raised by the evidence,
"a reasonable doubt on the issue requires that the defendant
be acquitted."[52]

The Supreme Court of Texas recently addressed the use
of certain secular terms by Tyndale Theological Seminary
and Bible Institute, a ministry of HEB Ministries, Inc., a
church in Fort Worth, Texas.[53] In that case,

> a law in the State of Texas required a private post-secondary
> school to meet prescribed standards before it may call itself a
> "seminary" or use words like "degree", "associate",
> "bachelor", "master", and "doctor" — or their equivalents —
> to recognize attainment in religious education and training.
> Violation of the law was a Class A misdemeanor and was also
> punishable by a civil penalty of $1,000 per day. The issue was
> whether this requirement impermissibly intrudes upon
> religious freedom protected by the United States and Texas
> Constitutions.
>
> HEB ministries was fined $173,000 for violating the law.
> The Texas Supreme Court ruled in favor of HEB ministries.
>
> HEB contended that "the State cannot deny the use of such
> higher education terminology to religious schools that do not
> meet its standards."
>
> The court stated, among other important pronouncements,
> that

---

[50] Texas Penal Code § 9.02 (2007).
[51] *Ibid.*, § 9.31 (2007).
[52] *Ibid.*, § 2.03(d) (2007).
[53] *HEB Ministries, Inc. v. Texas Higher Education Coordinating Board*, __S.W.3d__
(Tex. 2007).

> "[T]he government cannot set standards for religious education or training." ... "Neutrality is what is required. The State must confine itself to secular objectives, and neither advance nor impede religious activity." ... [S]etting standards for a religious education is a religious exercise for which the State lacks not only authority but competence." ... "By restricting the terminology a religious institution can use, the State signals its approval or disapproval of the institution's operation and curriculum as vividly as if it hung the state seal on the institution's front door."[54]

The pastor/trustee who holds property for the benefit of the Lord, since he holds that property in sacred trust for the Lord, is not to utilize the property as a profit-making venture in any way. The purpose of holding the property is to glorify God by allowing the church to assemble together to worship and glorify God. This does not mean that the pastor/trustee, upon consultation with other members of the church body, cannot sell the property at an appreciated price. All proceeds from a sale of such property, no matter the sales price, should be used for the glory of God. Since the pastor must meet the highest of biblical standards, he is least likely, of all church members, to deal carelessly or in a sinful manner in carrying out his responsibilities.

---

[54] *Ibid.*

Chapter 8
Spurious rationale for corporate-501(c)(3) status: tax exemption and tax deduction for contributions

As was shown in Chapter 4, page 38, according to IRS Code § 508, churches are an exception to the 501(c)(3) filing requirement. The IRS explicitly recognizes that religious organizations under 501(c)(3), to avoid paying taxes, must file for exempt status and that churches which do not file for exempt status under 501(c)(3) are non-taxable:

> "Unlike churches, religious organizations that wish to be tax exempt generally must apply to the IRS for tax-exempt status unless their gross receipts do not normally exceed $5,000 annually."[1]

Why then do churches seek 501(c)(3) tax exemption? The IRS gives the answer:

> "Although there is no requirement to do so, many churches seek recognition of tax-exempt status from the IRS because such recognition assures church leaders, members, and contributors that the church is recognized as exempt and qualifies for related tax benefits. For example, contributors to a church that has been recognized as tax exempt would know that their contributions generally are tax-deductible."[2]

Will the IRS disallow a tax deduction for gifts to a New Testament Church? The IRS Code § 170 provides:

> "§ 170. Charitable, etc., contributions and gifts....
> (a) Allowance of deduction.
> "(1) General rule. There shall be allowed as a deduction any charitable contribution (as defined in subsection (c)) payment of which is made within the taxable year. **A charitable contribution**

---

[1] IRS Publication 1828 (2007), p. 3. The publication is not the law, but just a comment on the law.
[2] *Ibid.*

shall be allowable as a deduction only if verified under regulations prescribed by the Secretary. [Emphasis mine.]
"(c) Charitable contribution defined. For purposes of this section, the term 'charitable contribution' means a contribution or gift to or for the use of—

'(2) A corporation, trust, or community chest, fund, or foundation-

'(A) created or organized in the United States or in any possession thereof, or under the law of the United States, any State, the District of Columbia, or any possession of the United States;

'(B) organized and operated exclusively for religious, charitable, scientific, literary, or educational purposes, or to foster national or international amateur sports competition (but only if no part of its activities involve the provision of athletic facilities or equipment), or for the prevention of cruelty to children or animals;'

"(C) no part of the net earnings of which inures to the benefit of any private shareholder or individual; and

"(D) which is not disqualified for tax exemption under section 501(c)(3) [26 USCS § 501(c)(3)] by reason of attempting to influence legislation, and which does not participate in, or intervene in (including the publishing or distributing of statements), any political campaign on behalf of (or in opposition to) any candidate for public office."[3]

The author has found only one case, a case from a federal district court in 1962, which addresses the issue of deductions for members of a New Testament church.[4] That case held that § 170 applies to what appears from the record to have been, at least for the most part, a New Testament church. The government argued that contributions did not qualify as deductions. The Court held for the church on all points. The government's arguments and the court's holdings follow:

"(1) The government argued that the church was not in fact an 'organized association as contemplated by the statute (no

---

[3] 26 U.S.C. § 170.
[4] *Morey v. Riddell*, 205 F. Supp. 918 (S.D. Cal. 1962).

distinctive identifying name, no written charter, constitution, bylaws, or operational guide other than the Holy Bible; it had no permanent headquarters, it did not maintain comprehensive records, and its funds were not held in a bank account designated as a church account.)

"Held. The members of the church regard themselves simply as members of the body of Christ (as following the teachings of Christ in the NT). They have no denominational name, no written organizational guide supplementary to the NT because they believe to do so would be to add an arbitrary gloss to biblical precepts, thus obscuring the word of God. Yet, in adherence to this philosophy, they have bound themselves together in an organized association. Many of them have worshipped together for years in furtherance of the purposes of the church. They hold regular public meetings in homes and rented quarters for Bible study, worship and evangelism. They assemble together in 'camp meetings'. As an association, they sponsor radio broadcasts and print and distribute Bible literature. They recognize specific individuals as ministers and as church officers, from whom they accept guidance. Through the years their ministers have regularly performed marriage ceremonies accepted as valid by civil authorities. Thus, while the church lacks some of the common indicia of organization, it plainly is an organized association of persons dedicated to religious purposes.

"(2) The government argued that the church was not organized in the U.S. as required by statute.

"Held. The basis for this contention is certain testimony that the church had its beginnings in Jerusalem in 33 A.D. It is perfectly obvious that what was meant by this testimony was that the Christian Church in the all-inclusive sense began in Jerusalem in 33 A.D. There is no doubt that the association constituting the church for whose use the contributions were made was organized in the United States.

"(3) the government argued that the church does not qualify as a beneficiary for deductible contributions because no showing has been made that in the event of its dissolution its assets would by operation of law be distributed solely for religious purposes.

"Held. This suggestion is prompted by [certain sections of the Income Tax Regulations and the C.F.R. that establish] that upon dissolution its assets must be distributable solely for an exempt purpose, either by terms of its articles of by operation of law. This regulation has no governing force in respect to the determination of the deductibility of plaintiffs' contributions for two reasons. It had not yet been promulgated at the time the contributions were made and tax returns filed.... The regulation ... is obviously intended as a safeguard against the possibility that funds accumulated by an organization by reason of its tax-exempt status might, in the event of its dissolution, be used for purposes other that those to which it was dedicated.... [See case for important part of the analysis.] It is evident that the contributions made by plaintiffs have long since been spent in furtherance of the religious purposes of the church, and that there is no possibility of their application to other uses.

"(4) The government argued that the contributions were made by checks payable to the order of four of the church's ministers.

"Held. The government cites several cases in which bequests inured to the benefit of the order. These cases are factually distinguishable because in each case the Court found that the testator intended to make the bequest to the named individual. In the present case, it is clear from the evidence that plaintiffs did not intend to make contributions to ministers, individually, but placed the funds in their hands, as agents, for the use of the church.

"(5) The government argued that the plaintiff's contributions were not deductible because they inured to the benefit of individuals (the church's ministers).

"Held. The individuals benefited were the church's recognized ministers, who employed a portion of the contributions given for the use of the church to pay their living expenses. Such use of the contributions does not constitute a departure from the statutory requirement that no part of the net profits of the organization shall inure to the benefit of any individual, for the sums expended to meet the living expenses of the ministers were no part of the net profits of the church. They were monies expended to meet legitimate expenses of the church in implementing its religious purposes. These expenses were of the same character as the salaries paid by any religious or charitable organization to its staff. The evidence was clear that the ministers devoted the major portion of their time to work of the church and that the amount of church funds used to pay their modest living expenses was small in comparison to the extent of their services."[5]

In line with the above case and the First Amendment, the IRS agrees that contributions to a non-incorporated, non-501(c)(3) church are deductible.

"You can deduct contributions only if you make them to a qualified organization. **To become a qualified organization, most organizations, other than churches and governments, as described below, must apply to the IRS**.... You can ask any organization whether it is a qualified organization, and most will be able to tell you. Or you can check IRS Publication 78 which lists most qualified organizations. You may find Publication 78 in your local library's reference section. Or you can find it on the internet at *www.irs.gov*. You can also call the IRS to find out if an organization is qualified. Call 1-877-829-5500...."[6] [Bold emphasis mine.]

However, the above does not tell the whole story. Other regulations come into play and definitely affect the ability and desirability of seeking tax deductions for contributions by a member of a New Testament church. Another reason some churches seek 501(c)(3) status is that IRS regulations make it more difficult for members to receive tax deductions for tithes and offerings to a New Testament church than to an incorporated 501(c)(3) religious organization.

"A donor cannot claim a tax deduction for any single contribution of $250 or more unless the donor obtains a contemporaneous, written acknowledgment of the contribution from the recipient church or religious organization. A church or religious organization that does not acknowledge a contribution incurs no penalty; but without a written acknowledgment, the donor cannot claim a tax deduction."[7]

---

[5] *Ibid.* All matters concerning tax deductions for contributions to churches are not covered. For a complete overview, see the cited publications.
[5] IRS Publication 526 (2007), pp. 2-3.
[7] IRS Publication 1828 (2007), p. 20.

To receive a deduction, one must have records to prove his contributions. For cash contributions less than $250, he must keep one of the following:

"1. A cancelled check, or a legible and readable account statement that shows:
  "a. If payment was by check—the check number, amount, date posted, and to whom paid,
  "b. if payment was by electronic funds transfer—the amount, date posted, and to whom paid, or
  "c. if payment was charged to a credit card—the amount, transaction date, and to whom paid.
"2. A receipt (or a letter or other written communication) from the charitable organization showing the name of the organization, the date of the contribution, and the amount of the contribution.
"3. Other reliable written records that include the information described in (2). Records may be considered reliable if they were made at or near the time of the contribution, were regularly kept by you, or if, in the case of small donations, you have buttons, emblems, or other tokens, that are regularly given to persons making small cash contributions. "[Provisions are made for car expenses]."[8]

"Beginning in 2007, you cannot deduct a cash contribution, regardless of the amount, unless you keep a bank record (such as a cancelled check, a bank copy of a canceled check, or a bank statement containing the name of the charity, the date, and the amount) or a written communication from the qualified organization. The written communication must include the name of the organization, the date of the contribution, and the amount of the contribution."[9]

For contributions of more than $250, one must keep one of the following:

"You can claim a deduction for a contribution of $250 or more only if you have an acknowledgement of your contribution from the qualified organization or certain payroll deduction records.

---

[8] IRS Publication 526 (2007), p. 18.
[9] *Ibid.*

"If you claim more than one contribution of $250 or more, you must have either a separate acknowledgement for each or one acknowledgement that shows your total contributions."[10]

"Acknowledgement. The acknowledgement must meet these tests.
"1. It must be written.
"2. It must include:
"a. The amount of cash you contributed.
"b. Whether the qualified organization gave you any goods or services as a result of your contribution (other than certain taken items and membership benefits), and
"c. A description and good faith estimate of the value of any goods or services described in (b). If the only benefit you received was an intangible religious benefit (such as admission to a religious ceremony) that generally is not sold in a commercial transaction outside the donative context, the acknowledgement must say so and does not need to describe or estimate the value of the benefit.
"3. You must get it on or before the earlier of:
"a. The date you file your return for the year you make the contribution, or
"b. The due date, including extensions, for filing the return.[11]

"Payroll deductions. If you make a contribution by payroll deduction, you do not need an acknowledgement from the qualified organization. But if your employer deducted $250 or more from a single paycheck, you must keep:
"1. A pay stub, Form W-2, or other document furnished by your employer that proves the amount withheld, and
"2. A pledge card or other document from the qualified organization that states the organization does not provide goods or services in return for any contribution made to it by payroll deduction.

"Beginning in 2007, you must keep the records just described for any contribution by payroll deduction, regardless of amount. However, the pledge card or other document must

---

[10] *Ibid.*
[11] *Ibid.*

include the statement described in (2) regarding goods and services only if your employer withheld $250 or more from a single paycheck."[12]

"Out of pocket expenses....
"Noncash contributions (rules given for noncash contributions depend on the value of the contributions.) ..."[13]

Also, according to the IRS, a church may assist the IRS and issue written statements for gifts of $250 or more given the church, which will be honored by the IRS if such receipts contain the following information:

"the name of the church or religious organization; date of contribution; amount of any cash contribution, and description (but not the value) of non-cash contributions; statement that no goods or services were provided by the church religious organization in return for the contribution; statement that goods or services that a church or religious organization provided in return for the contribution consisted entirely of intangible religious benefits, or description and good faith estimate of the value of goods or services other than intangible religious benefits that the church or religious organization provided in return for the contribution.

"The church or religious organization may either provide separate acknowledgments for each single contribution of $250 or more or one acknowledgment to substantiate several single contributions of $250 or more. Separate contributions are not aggregated for purposes of measuring the $250 threshold."[14]

Again, a New Testament church as a spiritual entity cannot hold any type of property, including money, nor can she issue receipts. Therefore, one cannot give anything to a New Testament church. However, money given for a certain purpose directly to the recipient, or money given a person such as a pastor/trustee who holds property for the benefit of the Lord Jesus Christ for a certain purpose or

[12] *Ibid.*
[13] *Ibid.*, pp. 18-19.
[14] IRS Publication 1828 (2007), p. 20.

purposes is different. A pastor/trustee, in the opinion of the author, can give a thank you letter to a person who gave money for a certain purpose when the money was used for the purpose given. The letter cannot indicate that the gift was given to the church, since a church cannot hold or own money or any kind of property.

Furthermore, how can a New Testament church keep records of any kind since she is a spiritual, not an earthly, entity? Only those who have been born again are members of a church and only God adds to the church those who have been saved. God surely keeps records of those who are wheat in His churches. How can a New Testament church know for sure who is saved and therefore keep records of church membership?

IRS regulations require that:

> "All tax-exempt organizations, including churches and religious organizations (regardless of whether tax-exempt status has been officially recognized by the IRS), are required to maintain books of accounting and other records necessary to justify their claim for exemption in the event of an audit."[15]

The Bible contains no example of our Lord or a church keeping financial records. Judas stole from the money bag he carried.[16] No apostle made an issue of it. Christ, as omniscient God, knew about it, but did not rebuke him in any way or turn Judas in to the civil authority. No instructions for a church to keep financial records can be found in the New Testament. Would not keeping records require a church to behave somewhat like a business, thereby destroying her status as a spiritual entity?

In addition, "charitable contribution" under IRC § 170 quoted *supra* at page 53, means "a contribution or gift to or for the use of ... a corporation, trust, or community chest, fund, or foundation ... organized and operated exclusively

---

[5] *Ibid.*, p. 17.
[6] See Jn. 12.6.

for religious [or] charitable ... purposes ... which is not disqualified for tax exemption under section 501(c)(3) [26 USCS § 501(c)(3)] by reason of attempting to influence legislation, and which does not participate in, or intervene in (including the publishing or distributing of statements), any political campaign on behalf of (or in opposition to) any candidate for public office." A New Testament church may find that the Lord has directed the church to attempt to influence legislation or support or oppose a political candidate in violation of § 170. Can a New Testament church accept such limitations on her spiritual responsibilities?

Can a New Testament church have employees and conform to biblical principle? The author does not believe so. Do you agree? To have employees subjects the church to Federal Insurance Contributions Act (FICA) taxes which consist of Social Security and Medicare taxes:[17]

> Wages paid to employees of churches or religious organizations are subject to FICA taxes unless: (1) wages are paid for services performed by a duly ordained, commissioned, or licensed minister of a church in the exercise of his or her ministry, or by a member of a religious order in the exercise of duties required by such order, (2) the church or religious organization pays the employee wages of less than $108.28 in a calendar year, or (3) a church that is opposed to the payment of social security and Medicare taxes for religious reasons [files Form 8274].... If such an election is made, affected employees must pay Self-Employment Contributions Act (SECA) tax...."[18]

Unlike exempt organizations or businesses, civil law provides that a church is not required to withhold income tax from the compensation that it pays to its duly ordained, commissioned, or licensed ministers for performing

---

[17] IRS Publication 1828, p. 14.
[18] *Ibid.*

services in the exercise of their ministry.[19] The author believes that a New Testament church cannot "compensate" or pay wages to anyone, and at the same time remain in conformity to biblical principle and remain a spiritual entity. A New Testament church cannot own property of any kind, including money.   Members as individuals can give to others—including a pastor/trustee who is to hold and distribute property for the benefit of the Lord Jesus Christ. Members can give gifts to their pastor for his support.

Other IRS rules apply to taxes on compensation of ministers. Can a New Testament church pay wages or any type of compensation to her pastor or anyone else? The author believes that the Bible teaches that members of New Testament church can give love gifts to take care of a pastor or to anyone, but those gifts are not wages and are not required by contract or any other earthly rule.

> "Nearly 30 years ago, an eminent minister insisted before Congress that: [T]he first amendment ... should not permit the state to tell the church when it is being 'religious' and when it is not. The church must be permitted to define its own goals in society in terms of the imperatives of its religious faith. Is the Christian church somehow not being religious when it works on behalf of healing the sick, or for the rights of minorities, or as peacemaker on the international scene? No, the church itself must define the perimeters of its outreach on public policy questions."[20]

A New Testament church is forever protected by God and presently by the First Amendment. On the other hand, a state incorporated church enters into a contract with the state, the sovereign of the corporation. An incorporated

---

[19] *Ibid.*, p. 15.
[20] Garnett, p., 772, citing *Legislative Activity By Certain Types of Exempt Organizations: Hearings Before the House Ways and Means Committee*, 92d Cong., 2d Sess. 99, 305 (1972) quoted in Edward McGlynn Gaffney, Jr., *On Not Rendering to Caesar: The Unconstitutionality of Tax Regulation of Activities of Religious Organizations Relating to Politics*, 40 DePaul L. Rev. 1, 20 (1990).

church assumes a second personality—that of an artificial person, a legal entity, capable of suing and being sued. Incorporation provides for civil governmental regulation in many areas, and it does not protect the church from all governmental interference with matters outside the contract. When a church seeks and acquires 501(c)(3) status, she thereby has agreed to certain restrictions and that she will abide by public policy. She also submits herself to anti-biblical teaching from civil government through the IRS. Most egregious of all, in the opinion of the author according to the Bible, she, like Israel who asked for a king, has committed a great wickedness against God and the results will prove to be undesirable.[21]

---

[21] See *God Betrayed...*, for consequences when a church becomes a legal entity.

Chapter 9
Conclusion

Pastors and Christians need to seriously look at the issues presented in this book. Incorporation subjects churches to an earthly head, the state, and requires churches to comply with earthly principles and procedures in many matters rather than God's biblical principles and procedures in all matters. Corporate trustees of incorporated churches conduct church matters according to contract principles; and, therefore, to one degree or another, they walk in the flesh and not in the spirit. Factually, the corporation, according to state law, owns the property utilized by the church. Incorporation also creates several contracts: between the contracting entities (the members of the incorporated church), between each contracting entity and the state (each church member and the state), between the entity thereby created and the state, and between the members inter se. In addition, the members own the corporation. The members/owners of the church, not the pastor, are the overseers, rulers, and trustees of the church, and the members/owners many times exercise their contractual powers given them by their sovereign state to control the pastor, even hiring or firing pastors at will.

IRC provisions have further entangled churches with civil government. Civil government has enticed almost all incorporated churches to become religious organizations under federal law, the IRC. The IRC presents an exemption-education-control scheme which most churches have not been able to resist. State help and state methods are designed to keep the gospel within the four walls of a building, and then to allow the civil government to enter those four walls. A corporate 501(c)(3) church grieves our Lord by placing herself under an additional head.

Churches must be careful to maintain their New Testament church status. They must also make sure that they do not inadvertently become legal entities through means other than incorporation and 501(c)(3).

Every born again believer should attempt to make sure that he and the church he attends honors the Lord Jesus in all things. God takes His relationships with His children individually and with His churches very seriously and He wants them to do likewise.

Lightning Source UK Ltd.
Milton Keynes UK
UKOW050808290112

186278UK00001B/16/P